Angels

AND COMPANIONS IN SPIRIT

LAEH MAGGIE GARFIELD
& JACK GRANT

CELESTIAL ARTS
BERKELEY, CALIFORNIA

CA Celestial Arts Publishing
P. O. Box 7123, Berkeley, California 94707

Cover design by Fifth Street Design, Berkeley, California.

Cover photo shows a detail of a panel from the south door of the Baptistery by Lorenzo Ghiberti in Florence, Italy.

Library of Congress catalog card number: 84-45362

Printed in the United States of America

First Printing, 1995

4 5 / 99

In memory of my aunt, Rose Spitzberg,
who raised me to see what service I
might do in the world;

and in memory of Essie Parrish,
Pomo shaman, who taught me to trust
my own healing and visionary power.

Laeh Maggie Garfield

For all of you who, like myself,
are skeptics as well as explorers,
and who would rather have practical
information for personal experiment
than doctrinal explanations and pat
answers.

Jack Grant

Believe nothing on the faith of traditions, even
though they have been held in honor for many generations
and in divers places. Do not believe a thing because
many people speak of it. Do not believe on the faith
of the sages of the past. Do not believe what you
yourself have imagined, persuading yourself that
a God inspires you. Believe nothing on the sole authority
of your masters or priests. After examination, believe
what you yourself have tested and found to be reasonable,
and conform your conduct thereto.

Gautama Buddha

FOREWORD

by Laeh Maggie Garfield

This book is the outgrowth of experiences I've had since I was a small girl. Contact with guides has always been easy for me. At the age of seven, I used to play with numerous spirit companions, not realizing that most people limit themselves to one or two such relationships, if any. I *was* aware that most children sever themselves from their guides due to adult pressure. But in my case—even in a large extended family—this wasn't necessary. I often overheard family members speak of someone who'd been able to stay in contact with a friend or relation who had passed on; this was not considered a mystery or something exotic. After the death of my paternal grandmother when I was twelve, I fully expected to experience her presence again. Nor was I disappointed, for she came to me in dreams with important messages. When I reported these messages—and other messages—no one in the family ever laughed at me or told me that these communications weren't real.

My Aunt Rose taught me to read natural signs, to interpret the deeper levels of events that "happen" to people, and to understand old-fashioned methods of healing. She consistently approved of my efforts to seek and learn in the spiritual realm. At the age of five and a half I'd been near death during a major illness, and it was Aunt Rose who pulled me back. She knew that, thereafter, ordinary religious answers wouldn't be enough to satisfy all my questions. She was right. I simply couldn't believe what short-sighted people tried to tell me about God or our purpose here on earth. The dual focus of Aunt Rose's informal teaching was to acquaint me with my own purpose and to give me a background in the details of its practice.

With college and a marriage, I let some of this knowledge lie dormant. I still had a definite sense of purpose, however, and continued to develop certain skills. Throughout the early 1970s, when I was in my late twenties, I studied with Essie Parrish, the Pomo shaman. Mrs. Parrish taught me how to work with "helping spirits," and how to use different sounds to call them for different kinds of assistance.

Then, in 1976, my marital situation broke up over a period of months. At the time I felt all but incapacitated with grief. But in fact I was going through a series of intense changes, each of which generated challenges and demanded personal growth. One of these changes concerned my connections with spirit guides. Although close to my life guide and several other spirit helpers, I was surprised by the appearance of new guides as well as the reappearance of entities who had passed through my life in years previous. It seemed that the universe was going to care for me and see to it that I moved on to the next stage of my life path. As a corollary to this influx of support, my worldly needs were met by the kind people of Horton Valley, Oregon, who became my neighbors that summer.

I was still feeling distraught, however. At a friendly hardball game on the Fourth of July I broke my left thumb, an indication that my insight was being adversely affected by the emotional drain. This was true. My dreams were empty, my waking inspirations nil. I was fortunate to be getting the extra guided input.

That very day, as I searched for comfrey leaves to hasten the reknitting of the broken bone, there suddenly arrived an entity who gave the name Marie Le Casteau. As she does even now, she wore a beekeeper's bonnet with heavy netting around it. Though I couldn't see her face, her warm gentle presence was a comfort. She had come not only to soothe my grief but to help me toward fullness in my career, in part by putting together an easy-to-understand book on how to contact spirit guides and interact with them.

As 1976 drew to a close, some Horton Valley friends saw an ad in the paper for a staff opening at the Eugene Center for Personal Growth. With their encouragement I applied for the position and, though I didn't look like the typical therapist, was taken on as a member. Other practitioners at the center held workshops on weekends. It wasn't long before Johannah, my most frequent spirit companion, and Marie Le Casteau suggested a weekend seminar in which they could publicly participate. We called it simply "Working with Your Spirit Guides."

While I had privately introduced people to their guides for years, I was concerned that it might be difficult to do this in a group setting. Nevertheless, the first workshop at the center was a success. All the material I needed was provided by my spirit helpers. More workshops followed, no two of them exactly alike. The basic information and the exercises for meeting a guide remained the same, but each presentation was tailored to the questions and the developmental level of the particular group.

After the workshops were under way, people would occasionally stop me on the street or take me aside at a party to confide that they had contacted their guides one or more times, but were secretive about them for fear of being thought mentally unbalanced. Some expressed the hope that a sensible book on the subject might help to cast their experiences with spirit companions in a more socially acceptable light. Meanwhile many of the workshop participants and my other clients requested that I recommend a suitable book that they could take home and study. Unfortunately, I could not. The only material I'd been able to find in print was either mystical, impractical, or downright foolish.

Now I was also feeling pressure from my guides. They kept pouring in the information. In early 1978 I taped a workshop. A couple of clients offered to trade healings in exchange for transcribing the tapes, and my apprentice volunteered to edit the transcript.

The verbal flow of a workshop is based on group interaction, eye contact, and other visual stimulation, and this one went well. But turned into word-for-word prose, it seemed awkward and repetitive—and, in other places, too sketchy. Information in written form must be linear and clear, spare and meaningful. I realized that, even with editing, the tape transcript was far from adequate as the groundwork for a book, and that to organize a quality book-length manuscript was more than my free time would permit. I saw clients during the days, taught several nights a week, gave local or out-of-town seminars on weekends, and kept a home as a single parent in sole custody of two children.

For a year I let the transcript sit while I looked for a co-author—somebody who respected intuition or inner teaching, but contentious enough to challenge my material and help me bring it to greater clarity. I also wanted to learn more about the writing and rewriting process so that I might do better with it myself in the future. To find the right person was a tall order. Thus far I'd drawn a blank.

In the latter part of 1978, thanks to an attractive job opportunity and certain advantages for my children, I decided to resettle temporarily in Northern California. Spring of 1979 found me in the throes of moving from one house to another. Since my new place wasn't quite ready for occupancy, some friends invited me and my daughters to stay in a cabin on the ten acres they had recently purchased. It was a hectic weekend. I had two workshops to give, was trying to move, and was also preparing to go on a long-planned family vacation with my brother. Racing down the dirt access road to my friends' property, I turned into the wrong driveway. There I was met and redirected by an effervescent woman named Ann Grant. I noticed she had a son in the same age bracket as my friends' son, so I suggested that the boys—and the moms—get acquainted.

Although I didn't know it at the time, there was another entity in addition to Marie Le Casteau who had been pulling strings to ensure that the spirit-guide book would get written. This was White Eagle, a master guide. As I later found out, White Eagle was making doubly sure that a certain hookup would take place. While I was on vacation a man named Jack Grant called the office and made an appointment for a past-life regression. Upon my return, I noted the appointment but did not connect his name with that of the woman I'd encountered on the driveway.

And then one day soon afterward, as we were sitting around the front room of my friends' house, Ann Grant came by for a first visit. In the course of conversation I heard her say that her husband Jack, a writer, had just turned down an offer to collaborate on a book with a psychic because, although he was interested in the subject, he didn't like the publisher's terms. The terms he wanted seemed reasonable enough to me—as a matter of fact, they were the same terms I'd been planning to extend to *my* co-author—and all at once I was struck by the certainty that Jack was the very person I'd been looking for in this regard. I asked Ann to please call him and introduce us.

Jack was rather reticent, but I stopped by his house and gave him a copy of the workshop transcript. His reaction was mixed. When I stopped in again a few days later, he said, "Well, this is nowhere near a finished product. My feeling is, set it aside and start afresh. But I do think you've got a book in you." And in return he gave me two things to read, a book that he had written (*The Ins and Outs of Soccer*, Prentice Hall) and one that he had extensively edited. I liked the straightforward, positive approach of both.

After Jack had considered my offer for a while and had gone through a workshop and a couple of past-life sessions, we agreed that we had a deal. I wanted to begin right away, but he was busy repairing the roof of his house and doing another writing project, and couldn't start until autumn. The summer went by quickly. In September we began meeting for three hours each Monday and Wednesday morning, usually at Jack's place, where it was quiet and therefore easy for me to stay grounded while channeling. Of course, I wasn't always channeling. There were stories to relate—reports from friends and former students and past experiences of my own. But it was important that the channeled material come out smoothly. And most of the time it did. In general, it took only a mild trance for me to merge with and interpret the thoughts that the guides were sending. Jack respected the rhythm of my channeling and didn't interrupt to excess, but he wasn't reluctant to step in now and then and ask for clarification. When he asked a question, I was able to remain fully cognizant of what the guide had just said, answer Jack as myself, and then shift back into the guide's energy field.

Despite an awareness of what was going on, Jack was all business, unruffled when the channeling was *not* going well. This happened one time when a rather autocratic entity was speaking through me. Although he'd been famous in his lifetime and had so far supplied me with some good information, he was bossy and inconsiderate. His energy was often oppressively heavy, and he even hinted that he'd like to drink brandy and smoke cigars while in my body. I was torn. I wanted the information, but I didn't want to pay the price of staving off his intrusive efforts. Seeing my distress, Jack asked after its cause. When I told him, he said, "I don't care who he is. You know the rules; throw him out." So I did, and this cleared a space. Thereupon Marie Le Casteau and Carole Judge came in to channel the concluding chapter of the book in a single sitting.

A year later I moved home to Oregon, and we had to revamp our methods. Sometimes the guides kept me up until 2 and 3 A.M. writing longhand. After a spirit-guide workshop, feeling inspired by the reactions and questions of the participants, I always came away with fresh ideas to add to the manuscript. Occasionally Jack or I would find a gap in a chapter, and a couple of times we felt that a sub-chapter deserved to be a chapter by itself. When this happened, we'd do our best separately and then compare notes by mail. I spent hours looking through old journals for relevant anecdotes, and talked on the phone with numerous people who had attended workshops and had interesting stories to tell.

Since I continued to return periodically to California, every three or four months Jack and I were able to spend a few concentrated days working on the chapters that needed expansion and going over the material that we'd mailed back and forth. Though we argued certain points, for the most part the process reflected our mutual good will. By this time our styles and viewpoints had reached a satisfactory level of consensus and the book was making progress. Some chapters we felt comfortable with and left largely alone even during final revisions. Others we sweated over from first to last.

As driven as I was to complete the manuscript, I can't at present explain the extent of this urgency. The ideas and the prodding I received from the guides were major incentives, but there was also a strong sense of commitment that rose up in me of its own accord. For so long the project was so much the bone and fiber of my existence. Now that it's behind me, my passion has already diminished, and I find it hard to expound rationally on what pressed me.

This past spring I sat on a river bank in Bremgarten, Switzerland. I was leading a workshop called "The Healing Power of Sound." While the people in the group meditated on the sound of the water, I took a moment to meditate too. Marie Le Casteau came to tease me about having managed to get me to Switzerland, her former home. She knew I'd be happy there, and I was. It seems that my spirit companions always know what I need to risk in order to take the next step. May your guides be just as good to you.

FOREWORD

by Jack Grant

In the spring of 1979 I became curious to attempt a past-life regression and began looking for an experienced coach. An acquaintance suggested Laeh Maggie Garfield, then living in our county in Northern California. The acquaintance said that Laeh had a good reputation for individual counseling as well as teaching group classes in various aspects of psychic work. I called up her office, talked to her secretary, and made an appointment.

Meanwhile Laeh was taking steps to move from one house to another within the county. For the time being, she had arranged to use a cabin belonging to our new neighbors across the creek. En route to their place she took a wrong turn and ended up in our driveway, where she met my wife Ann.

Three weeks later, I got a call from Ann, who was next door. She said, "There's a lady here who wants to make you a business offer," and proceeded to introduce Laeh. Recognizing the name, I thought at first that Laeh wanted to work out some sort of trade in connection with the past-life appointment. When it dawned on me that she had in mind a book-length project, my reaction was mostly negative. At one time or another I've probably been approached by a hundred needy people wanting me to "help out a little" with their prospective books. In this case I hadn't even met the person, so I was extra-leery—all but hostile, in fact. Besides, I'd already had a couple of unpleasant experiences—one personal, one financial—as the result of previous co-authoring efforts. I'd pretty much sworn off such arrangements forever. And I had three books of my own calling to me siren-like for attention whenever I neglected them too long.

On the other hand, Laeh's offer was undeniably fair, an indication she understood the amount of work that would be involved. Nor was she on some death-defying schedule, in order to jump into print. It's self-punishment to hurry your own book from inspiration and experience into final draft, self-torture to hurry a book which depends largely on the inspirations and experiences of someone else.

So I said, with about one percent conviction, that I'd consider it. At the past-life session we'd discover whether or not we hit it off as personalities. I also wanted to attend an upcoming spirit-guide workshop and see for myself.

The past-life session was vivid and illuminating. And at the workshop I did see for myself. Both experiences were an enjoyable surprise. I've been a meditator for almost fifteen years, and a lifelong recipient of verbal phrases and lines of song, but except in dreams I'm unaccustomed to receiving definite, lasting pictures with the inner eye.

I was still nowhere near saying yes to taking on the book, feeling that I had scarcely enough time and energy for my own projects. One of these projects, latent though not yet current, was a stage version, from a post-1970s perspective, of the life of Joan of Arc. Over the past several years I'd scribbled down and collected perhaps forty pages of idea-notes and conversation fragments that had flashed into my mind unbidden. And some of these conversations were between Joan and her guardian angels. Joan saw her guides regularly and spoke with them even more regularly. Since they played such an instrumental role in her affairs of this world, I thought they deserved to be on stage for the sake of realism.

Yet I could understand why other writers had chosen to leave them hovering in the wings. Some felt that anything between Joan and God was a private matter. Some considered her spirit contacts the fancy of an unsophisticated mind, and of minor importance to her story. Some may have preferred not to upset rationalist audiences with a "side issue." And some must have felt that they just didn't know enough about the subject to presume to make good dialogue of it. This last was my cause for hesitation. No sense presenting guides who weren't at least somewhat true to form.

In the course of mulling things over, I visited my sister, herself an actress and playwright. She urged me to work on the Joan piece if I felt ready for it. I said I did, except...And then it occurred to me very clearly that assisting with a book on spirit guides might genuinely serve a double purpose. Back home, I accepted Laeh's offer.

The mechanics of doing the book were fairly uncomplicated. To start with, I took down a rudimentary list of the many facets of spirit-guide work that Laeh wished to cover. (These would obviously be future chapters and chapter sections.) In anticipation of when we next got together, I suggested she think out at least one of these facets in detail, and be prepared to narrate her thoughts.

Evidently Laeh had indeed been contemplating the subject, because her thoughts proved to be in pretty good order, with illustrative anecdotes attached. But she didn't start out with Chapter One, page one. My procedure was to have her speak in measured phrases, as if dictating to a slow secretary—which I am. I wrote it all down in long-hand scrawl. This spared me the boring, time-consuming process of transcribing from a tape recorder and left me rough draft to look at later. The wording, having been delivered with care, was more concise and precise than most tape-recorded talk, which runs toward repetition and off-the-subject rambling, with too few pauses long enough for the formulation of editorial questions and comments. It was important not to interrupt Laeh's narrative flow, but sometimes it was better to deal with sentences and paragraphs as they arrived—discuss them, clarify them, or slug our way testily through them.

In between chunks of dictation, and occasionally in mid-stream, Laeh liked to break into a joke or ramble off on some unrelated story —partly her way of relaxing and making merry in order to renew her forces, partly writer escapism. I couldn't take offense since I do a certain amount of sidetracking and wandering in my own work, but as a co-writer I tend to be more ruthlessly focused.

For the next year or so, we met at frequent intervals for dictation sessions. I began to organize the chunks, fiddle with the prose details, and ask Laeh for missing pieces. After she moved back to Oregon, I started filling in some of the holes myself. I can't say that the source was a narrating entity, but since I realize that we're able to act as conduits and not just as walled-off integers, I was often impressed by the insistence and definition with which certain information presented itself. By mail, Laeh then corroborated or amended my additions.

Since this book is mainly by way of Laeh, the "I" in the remainder of the text refers to her. "Healing with Your Guide" came almost straight from her dictation. "Auras and Chakras" went through half a dozen difficult drafts, with input from us both. As devil's advocate, I contributed a fair amount to "Questions and Quandaries." Laeh supplied most of "Messages and Their Interpretation," except for the section on auditory channeling. The book as a whole has undergone three major overhauls, not to mention hundreds of small, last-minute revisions and a further editing job by Judy Johnstone. I think the net product is better for having taken this long.

Oh, yes. I finished *Joan Rainbow* last year. It's making the rounds of the new-play competitions and, judging by the response so far, I think it will find its place. And the guides are right there, big as life, alongside the Maid.

CONTENTS

1
OPEN SECRETS

In structure as well as in content, this book is primarily the result of observing what people need in order to work with spirit guides on their own. The material is designed to help you overcome skepticism and to validate contacts you may have already had.

There are forces in the universe that many of us barely understand. Since we don't understand these forces, we tend to be afraid or disdainful of them. Given correct information in plain language, however, almost all of us can couple this data with events from our own lives and thus begin to see that our material world is only one of numerous worlds that touch and interpenetrate.

Spirit beings are as interested in us as we are in them, if not more so. They're interested in our physical world and in us as individuals. They hold us in the light and love of the cosmos, and they have just the right vantage on our position to be excellent teachers and helpers. They can assist us to center our creativity, to attract abundance, to find what we desire nonmaterially, and to cultivate liberating qualities such as tolerance and forgiveness. In return we can do a great deal for them, not by giving up our integrity, but by treating them as they treat us: with consideration and respect.

If you believe that discarnate beings are out to siphon human power, you'll be glad to learn how to set limits on spirit relationships so that, as with human friends, you can cooperate on an equal basis.

Each chapter of this book shows how you can remain true to yourself while interacting with a guide.

Members of the spirit realm are not powerless themselves, of course. At times they're capable of independently opening up to you. It's just as true, however, that you are capable of initiating contact with them. People who think that the greater power belongs to the "dead" demean the capacities and strengths of incarnate life.

Though purity and saintliness often lead to uncommon sense-perceptions, you need not be a saint yourself before you can properly start to learn the so-called secrets of the universe. Working with spirit helpers is one of the more accessible "secret powers." Love is the highest and most accessible force of all.

A vivid encounter with a spirit being may be treated as an isolated achievement, an end in itself. The deeper value of such an encounter, however, is that it can enable you to become clearer about the behavior patterns and the reality structures you've made in your physical life. One of the main reasons spirits contact us is to help us understand that this earthly existence is not all there is. Thus equipped, we may act, while still on earth, according to the larger perspective that comes from this knowledge.

Your guides are your protectors. They can save you from hazards, predicaments and unhealthy pursuits. They can also help to alleviate the heaviness of a serious situation. A midwife I know feels a tremendous energy come over her when she's attending a birth. One time I went to a birth as her assistant. What she sensed as an influx of birthing energy I perceived as the arrival of her guide.

Our history and literature are replete with instances of people receiving information and inspiration from beyond. Socrates had his *daemon*. Jacob Boehme and Emanuel Swedenborg were instructed by spirit companions. William Blake received artistic guidance from his departed brother Robert and several other discarnates. Gilbert Murray, the eminent translator of Greek classics, mentions "a Friend behind phenomena," which is experienced either as a personal spirit of great wisdom or as the indestructible core of one's being.

Ancestor worship is perhaps the most common form of spirit-guide contact. All over the world, psychics entrusted with community welfare call upon ancestors—and not merely biological ancestors—to intercede with problems, bring visions and assist with healings. Among other cultures the Japanese have literalized and ritualized this form of petition.

Our particular society does not devote a lot of attention to dreams and mystical occurrences. Yet even among the societies that do, there's a tendency for priests of various sorts to keep important information occult. No matter what the prevailing attitude toward spiritual reality. there seem to be two kinds of religious people the world over. There are the orthodox ones, who accept the correctness of what they've been told and fear punishment for incorrectness; and there are the mystics, who believe according to their own experience and act on the basis of faith.

As Michael Harner, anthropologist and shaman, once said in a talk: "Along with the development of the state in different parts of the world, there was the development of certain dogmas associated with the state, and state religion evolved. Any time you have a prevailing ecclesiastical structure, it is rather threatening, both to officials and to orthodox followers, when someone claims to be in direct contact with a spirit or with a divine source, especially when the received wisdom doesn't coincide with the state's point of view. At various times in history shamans and saints have been persecuted by the state for their nonconforming beliefs about religion and reality."

Fortunately, this is not now the case in most nations of the world. We evolve globally as well as individually and regionally. At this point in our global evolution, we are learning magnanimity and absorbing compassion. (Compassion is the emotional component, magnanimity the intellectual component.) Insofar as we're able to be compassionate and magnanimous, we are all potential magi.

As the level of enlightened compassion continues to rise, the collective need for a priesthood of the knowledgable few diminishes. This kind of societal change seems to occur in relatively sudden bursts, as when the ecclesiastical rigidity of the Middle Ages gave way to the expansive developments of the Renaissance. Right now, if you travel to Toronto or Copenhagen or Athens or Rio or Bombay, you will find seekers and cultivators of truth, as well as sources of good information. Consider, for example, the worldwide wave of Tibetan Buddhists who have ventured forth to share, in simple language, secrets that used to be walled up within their monasteries.

Most of the powers customarily called occult or psychic are, in fact, abilities available to all of us. In hewing to conventional thought, we effective bar them not only from practical use but also from our consciousness. Even when we receive the most vital and pertinent information, we may deny it or allow it to slip away.

Some guides are impersonal disseminators of information. They bring down a poem or a piece of music and don't care where it lands. They just sing away to whoever might have an open channel. The result is that numerous variations on an invention may appear at roughly the same time, by way of individuals who were ready and willing to receive.

Most guides, however, are personal helpers and companions. A relationship with a guide is meant to be a form of interpersonal enrichment and enjoyment. Even though a guide may sometimes challenge you or irk you, your guide should be an entity about whom you generally feel enthusiastic and grateful. If not, you have the option of dismissing the ill-fitting spirit.

In his book *When Bad Things Happen to Good People* (Schocken Books, 1981), Rabbi Harold Kushner, who lost a son to progeria (accelerated aging), discusses the limits of what one can do in times of adversity. "The question we should be asking is not, 'Why did this happen to me? What did I do to deserve this?'. . . A better question would be 'Now that this has happened to me, what am I going to do about it?'" Rabbi Kushner advocates prayer, gratitude for a God who gives us strength to persevere and for the solace of friends who care, appreciation for life's greater good, and continuing effort to forgive and accept in love "a world which has disappointed you by not being perfect."

Approaching the same problem, Roman Catholic theologian Hans Kung speaks of God as "the Father who knows about everything in this far from perfect world and without whom nothing happens, whom man can absolutely trust, and on whom he can completely rely even in suffering, injustice, sin, and death."

These are both positive, inspired responses to the ache of loneliness and the agony of suffering. And so is the cultivation of a long-term relationship with a guide. Guides are representatives of God, intermediaries between the flesh-and-blood tangibility of human friends and ultimate union with the divine Source. When we're afflicted with grief or loneliness that doesn't go away in a congenial group, with a favorite book, or even with a dear friend or relative, our feelings stem from a longing for union with God, for the experience once again of unconditional love. Since guides are beings who reach out to us from the world of spirit, they're able to assuage our spiritual soreness in ways that human relationships and material comforts cannot.

At the same time, very few guides are angels. Angels are beings of an exalted order; for the most part their activity goes beyond the scope of everyday human concerns. Spirit guides are frequently termed *guardian angels*, but it's much more accurate to describe them as helpers and comforters, mentors and companions.

Though cautionary at times, this book is in no way intended to curb your own explorations. It is designed to get you started on a firm footing. It is also meant to spark your courage and imagination.

2
AURAS AND CHAKRAS

To feel balanced and at ease in the presence of your spirit guides, it is imperative that you learn how to control your own spiritual health. The aura around your body and the chakras within it are highly organized and concentrated configurations of life energy that are basic to each aspect of human existence—physical, mental, emotional, and spiritual. This chapter and the next deal with achieving inner stability and flexibility, so that you'll have a sense of freedom and control as you move between the earthly plane and the inspirational plane.

Auras

Most people who claim to see auras are actually able to discern only the innermost portion of the human energy field. This inner aura, which projects no more than six inches from the physical body, is referred to in religious mythology as the *halo* or *etheric body*.

The true aura extends at least four feet past your flesh-and-blood outline. At its apex, it rises thirty feet. Most out-of-body experiences are confined within this thirty-foot safety zone (for example, seeing oneself from above or from across the room). As long as your travels don't range beyond this, you can always return easily to your physical frame.

People who develop a sense of their own aura feel it in different ways. You may experience it as a cocoon of protective electricity, or as a warm private sea that surrounds you with gently flowing currents.

The brightness and clarity of your aura are clues to your overall state, including your physical well-being. Sensitive health practitioners may note auric details as an aid to diagnosing your condition. Dark splotches and empty spaces indicate present illness or physical trouble in the near future. A chronic ailment or a life crisis manifests its own peculiar quality of darkness. On the other hand, to the degree that your aura is intact and its colors are bright and luminescent, indications are that you enjoy health, stability, and security on all levels of existence. In general, the lighter and more luminescent one's auric hue, the more mature one's spiritual development.

Many of us do not build a full aura. For the most part, auric building and maintenance are done unconsciously. Since our society emphasizes the intellectual, we are likely to maintain a strong field around our heads and shoulders. Meanwhile, those of us who aren't naturally well-grounded tend to neglect the aura around the feet and ankles, or as far up as the knees. People with very poor grounding restrict their aura at their hips or even higher. It's a good practice to consciously visualize a complete, continuous auric field enveloping your body. Cultivation of an enlarged self-awareness will keep you safe and sane no matter who you're attempting to interact with, human or spirit.

Your aura influences and reflects your emotional, physical and mental presence. For spirit-guide work, a healthy aura is as important as the traditional "sound mind and sound body." If your aura is continuous and clear, and if its predominant color accords with the energetic hue that you wish to express in your life, you'll have no difficulty staying centered and sober while occupied with astral friends.

Although a healthy aura is often layered or interspersed with additional colors, or with several shades of the same color, the prevailing color you generate identifies the predominant quality of energy that you project and attract. Healthy auric colors are clear, pure, and translucent or luminescent. All colors, including off shades and three-color blends, can be found in human auras, but the dull, murky hues and certain dark colors are to be avoided, since they invite sickness and trouble.

The following are some of the connotative values attached to certain auric colors:

White (brilliant white, with a blue crystalline tinge, like fresh-fallen snow). The color of life essence, and therefore a sign of high spiritual attunement. As you move into an enlightened space, the colors that signal the event are sky-blue, gold, and crystal-white, usually in that order.

Silver. The color to use for triggering intuitive and creative channeling, including artistic endeavors such as music and writing. When you are done channeling, remove it and replace with your customary color.

Yellow. Intelligence, open-mindedness, inventiveness—the sustaining aspect of the life force. Yellow (life sustenance), blue (wisdom) and red (power) are the three primary colors and, at the moments of conception and birth, the three colors through which you burst into incarnate form.

Lemon-lime. Mentally soothing and uplifting. The consciousness is in the process of being elevated.

Gold. Sun-color; also one of the colors of newly risen consciousness and the hue of the highest earthly vibration regularly accessible. According to Eastern tradition, when you see gold during meditation, you have touched God—or, more precisely, the realm of archetypal creation.

Pumpkin orange (and all clear, golden oranges). One of the three universal healing colors. Denotes joy, vitality, abundance, and especially the ability to shape matter with your mind (to draw material goods and congenial people into your life).

Red. Strength, work, and activity. Bright red acts both as a stimulant and as a pain-reliever. However, since our society is already deluged by the type of energy this color releases, it is not recommended that you cultivate red in your aura or in your chakras.

Deep clear red. Sensuality, passion, or momentary anger.

Rose pink or *light pink.* Love and affection.

Orchid (pale blue-violet). Idealism.

Lavender. Sentimentality, nostalgia.

Magenta (red-violet). Self-exploration and inner vision, leading to compassion. Magenta fortifies intuitive ability.

Purple. Purification and transmutation; spiritual forcefulness. Useful when you're attempting to make a significant personal change, but don't overlook your physical body in the process.

Indigo (blue-violet). Soothing and cleansing. Helps control bleeding.

Amethyst (crystalline blue-purple). Deflects and purifies hostile vibrations coming toward you, so that you get only nurturing input.

Bright medium blue. Self-discipline, devotion, spiritual truth. Cools and relaxes the body; a sedative. Also generates confidence and the wisdom that comes with inner peace.

Sky blue. Peace and harmony with the universe. The color of the goodness that exists in every being; also the color to focus on when you want to feel at one with everything.

Turquoise. Another healing color. Attracts good luck and keeps mishaps from occurring.

Green. Balance, serenity, inner quiet. A universal healer and neutralizer, green promotes thorough grounding. In addition, green is the color of growing. When your aura is green, or stippled with green, you're *doing* the growing. The green fades into your new auric color as your growth begins to consolidate.

Light olive green. Another color that stimulates compassion and sympathy.

The remainder of the colors listed here are mentioned so that you may recognize them as undesirable elements in your aura. You're free to use them as reflective colors in your clothing and surroundings, but on the auric level they deserve to be transmuted, due to their clogging effect on the flow of body energy and emotional well-being.

Brown. An important color for improving your ability to organize your material world. Should be worn as clothing rather than put into the energy field. The same is true of beige and tan, which help you organize on the mental plane.

Rust (reddish brown or orange-brown). Either greed or a flair for attracting material wealth. Wear this color if you have trouble earning money or getting decent return for what you do.

Brick red. Deep-seated anger, the kind that doesn't go away no matter how many temperamental explosions you have.

Copper red. Repressed anger, often a mix of anxiety and jealousy. In Tibetan medicine, the astral color of cancer.

Red-orange. Produces a jangled vibration that feeds into survival fears and neurotic behavior patterns.

Navy blue. Dogmatism, rigid thinking.

Greyish green. Pessimism.

Pale grey. Fear.

Dark grey. A despondent morass.

Dull grey. Thorough depression and negativity. The angel of death is reputed to appear in this color.

Black. As a color that you wear, has certain uses for introspection and inner growth. Black causes a kind of sensory deprivation, so that you have a chance to look at your old data without being distracted by new material coming in. Black does attract negative energy, however. It's not good to wear frequently, and it's never under any circumstances to be introduced into your aura or chakras.

Chakras

Chakra is a Sanskrit word meaning "something that rotates." Chakras are rotating, conically shaped rays of energy, most of them centered along the body's vertical axis. Though nonmaterial, they can be felt—pulsing and pumping, or knotted and aching. They govern the physical functioning of your body, which is itself a configuration of swirling bits of highly energized matter. You mold and remold this matter into your self-image, based on your belief system of how you ought to appear. The blond child turns his hair brown with approaching adolescence. The straight-haired adolescent becomes a curly-haired adult. And we all believe in the gradual onset of old age; therefore we form wrinkles, grey hairs, liver spots, and other accepted signs of advancing years.

You create your own image, combining your self-perceptions with the information that other people feed you about yourself. Your chakras affect this process and are affected by it. "You're the luckiest kid I ever saw," your mother says; "What a super break," says your coach; and in both cases your first chakra swells in size. Thereafter your lucky breaks occur more regularly. Good fortune has become a trusted life pattern that you continue to draw into actuality through your enlarged first chakra, your bottommost major focus of swirling formative energy. This belief pattern enhances your ability to draw extra energy into your second and third chakras, and on up into each of your other major chakras in turn.

There are seven principal chakras (also called *centers* or *energy centers*) focused at least partly within the physical body. In addition, there are important chakras in the palms of your hands and the soles of your feet. This chapter is by no means intended to cover the entire subject of chakras. For the most part, it concentrates on information germane to practical success in working with a spirit guide.

The **first chakra**, also referred to as the *root chakra* or *kundalini center*, is the only major chakra whose larger opening is to the rear, just below the tailbone (the coccyx) and above the anus. There is a smaller opening in front, at the base of the pubic bone.

The first chakra has to do with your ability to survive, your capacity to have and hold, and your power to attract the abundance of the material realm into your life. When it's functioning properly you feel well, have great physical vitality, are comfortably grounded in your body, and are affectionate with the people close to you. If your physical self is chronically beset by aches and pains, if you don't get enough to eat, if the tax man takes too big a bite, if you're over-impulsive or always a little bit off-center, if you're liable to fits of cruelty or self-centered lust, then you're suffering from one of the typical problems that originate with (and reflect upon) an impeded first chakra.

Notice that even an external, impersonal affliction such as an excessive tax bill can be an indication that the "valve" of your first chakra has been somehow obstructed. When your first chakra is open, even if the city repaves the road in front of your house and assesses you for the expense, you get a timely pay raise or a windfall check to take care of the added burden.

Plutomania (materialistic greed) represents a first chakra that takes everything in but shares nothing and lets nothing go. Addiction to wealth coordinates with material envy, a third-chakra detriment, to form the darkest shadow-values of our culture. Someone with an open, balanced first chakra is materially confident and therefore generous.

The first chakra connects with the ovaries in women and the testes in men. Infertility and super-fecundity are malfunctions of first-chakra energy, relevant to survival of the species. The large intestine is another organ whose activity indicates first-chakra health. Constipation (over-attachment, the inability to let go) and diarrhea (compulsion to unload—situations, persons, conditions) are the extreme symptoms.

Although the first chakra has chiefly to do with survival, it also interrelates with your self-image, or with the image that you consistently fail to live up to. Family scripts, traditional life attitudes, and other deep-seated cues are implanted in our consicousness by way of the first chakra. Due to first-chakra programming, you may be a life-long child, wanting someone else to make everything all right. Or you may act like a perpetual teenager, overly idealistic and mad at the world.

Any dogma is an attack on the first chakra. Dogmatic preachers, parents and presiding authorities can get at you "where you live" and send your first chakra into a wobble. This may lead toward the eventual surrender of your self-governance.

The main purpose of a spirit guide is to help you take care of yourself. A guide's presence ought not to intrude upon your first chakra in any way. The cardinal rule of human/guide relationships is that *you* are in control. We all have the power both to summon our guides and to send them away.

The ideal size of a major chakra is about three inches in diameter as it enters the body. A person's first chakra may be quite a bit smaller than this, due to a contracted attitude toward being and feeling alive—

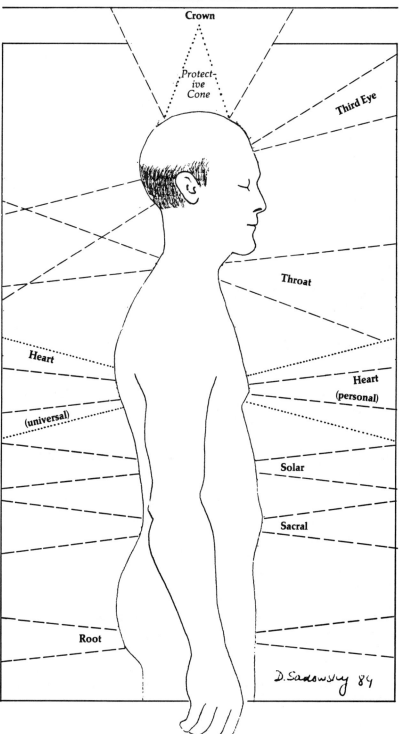

Crown

Protect-
ive
Cone

Third Eye

Throat

Heart

Heart
(personal)

(universal)

Solar

Sacral

Root

D. Sadowsky 84

or unhealthily larger, due to heavy materialism. It should be emphasized, however, that you don't diminish a larger chakra in order to open a smaller one. Your larger centers are those through which you presently deal with life. To try to shrink them could be damaging. The correct procedure is to concentrate on opening whichever chakras might be constricted or blocked. Then, as part of your overall rebalancing, the oversized chakras will diminish of their own accord.

The **second chakra,** also known as the *sacral center,* is located two inches below the navel and is the focus of your earliest and most fundamental emotions. Your basic sense of acceptance or rejection, worthiness or unworthiness; your sense of belonging to a group or family or of being alone in the world; your ease or trouble in connecting with God; all of these relate to how well your second chakra is working. Furthermore, through the spleen, the second chakra acts as a pumping mechanism for the physical energy the first chakra pulls in, and for the emotional energy to which it has access.

A healthy second is a sign of emotional integrity and security. You're optimistic, friendly, courageous, and sensitive to others' needs. You feel that you belong, and yet you're not afraid of being taken over when you merge with somebody else. If you have a difficult, unsatisfactory social life and have difficulty getting in touch with your own true feelings; if you're distressingly over-sensitive, or chronically bad-tempered and resentful, or prone to burying your emotions for months and then erupting with them; if you're often laid low by parental or religious guilt,[1] or immobilized by fears of injury, disapproval, isolation, or spirit possession, it is the second chakra that needs attention. An out-of-balance second sets off power-mongering in the third chakra and survival fears in the first. Its health is therefore pivotal in the physical realm.

The kidneys, which absorb and detoxify fear, and the spleen, which contains and processes worry, are both indicators of the second chakra's condition. So is the skin. Skin should be elastic—not puffy, or dry and scaly. In the same way, the boundaries of your emotional life should be resilient, neither bloated nor cracked and shrunken, so that you can make the changes required of you from day to day and year to year. When your second is fully functioning and discriminating, *clairsentience* (becoming one with another person) yields information that is presently useful and also prophetic.

---

[1]Watchdogs of morality, low on love because of a contracted second chakra, jump on other people who are exploring and enjoying the variety of life. Their efforts feed right into the guilt dysfunction.

You need to recognize and respect the emotions that move through your second chakra. It is also essential that you distinguish between your own feelings and those you pick up from others—repeatedly through close association, or haphazardly on the street or in a store. Be extra perceptive at parties, meetings, and mass gatherings. When necessary, be extra protective, so that you don't get drawn into an atmosphere of fear, depression, hysteria or violence.[2]

Failure to deal with the entire range of your emotional charges and to support their integrity invites paranoia and high blood pressure. Pancreatic ailments also reflect an undernourished second. Diabetes begins as fear of emotional neglect, escalating into fear of total abandonment, and may be handed on from parent to child when their energy fields intermingle.

At the opposite end of the emotional spectrum from fear is trust. Although trust relates to your dealings with others, it originates within yourself as a sense of security and personal validity. Don't worry about being able to trust others, be they humans or spirit helpers. Learn first of all to trust yourself: the desires that are heartfelt, the thoughts and actions that fullfill you, the responses that are emotionally satisfying.

If trust is a quality that you need to work on, make a request from the heart as you do the grounding and meditating exercise described in Chapter 3. Ask that you'll be able to demonstrate 2 percent more trust than you've shown during the past week. Do this over a period of time, and you'll find that you gradually grow into a more trusting and trustworthy individual.

The **third chakra** is the formative center of your personal power as a member of a social group, as well as the center of your capacity for getting along with the various others in this group. Also called the *solar plexus*, the third chakra is focused two to three inches above your navel. When your third is well-developed and unimpeded, you have plenty of physical stamina and resilience, plenty of self-control and self-respect. In general, you're able to channel energy into doing what you want, when you want.[3]

---

[2]There is little danger in picking up positive vibrations, feelings which elevate you. At the same time, if you have the gift of clairsentience, you must learn good grounding to compensate for explorations into the consciousness of other people and other beings.

[3]You're also unafraid to meditate, and the practice of meditation comes to you easily.

A poorly or negatively functioning third chakra produces inde-cisiveness and a sense of inadequacy, including the anxiety that people are out to take advantage of you. As compensation, you may become over-competitive, or you may suffer from possessive jealousy in regard to friends and lovers.

Some people have an excess of third-chakra energy which they abuse by trying to control others. The "bay windows" of Alfred Hitch-cock and Aristotle Onassis were bodily demonstrations of what hap-pens when third-chakra power is projected in a coercive or manipulative way. On the contrary, the gaunt figure bent over at the middle is someone who projects very little energy into the world, someone in dubious control of his own life.

The liver, which holds anger, the gall bladder, which has to do with decision-making abilities, and the stomach, which relates to the digestion of experience, are the organs whose proper functioning de-pends upon a well-regulated third chakra. Gallstones manifest a chronic denial of one's own best interest in order to please or placate another. Stomach problems indicate an inability to assimilate new ideas and beliefs, based on the fear that personal change will entail a loss of power. A well-toned muscle structure is also an indicator of the third chakra's health, and so is the blood, in terms of balanced cellular composition. When one's power center is functioning properly, the output of the adrenals produces no "rush" or undue stress.

With an open, active third chakra you enjoy self-respect. You value your own opinions without having to ram them down anyone else's throat. In social situations of your own choosing, you don't feel left out; you're able to participate fully without feeling impelled to kowtow or dominate. As an outgrowth of this, you radiate respect for other people.

We have inherited a mainstream of governmental tradition ac-cording to which a leader dictates the plan and the rest of the com-munity follows suit. Nonetheless, excellence of leadership consists in somehow coordinating everyone's strengths, skills and ideas so that all benefit, materially and spiritually. The true leader is able to steer each person into activity that contributes to his or her inner growth as well as the social good, thus creating real satisfaction. And loyalty. Loyalty is a function of a healthy third chakra. Blind obedience signals its negative functioning.

The same truth extends to your efforts at directing yourself. To win your own respect, you learn to manage and monitor your enthu-siasms without being tricky or repressive. You get yourself into activ-ities which exercise your talents and give you the pleasure of fulfill-

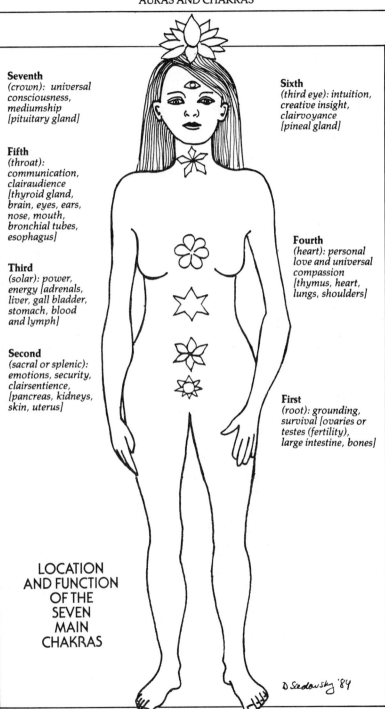

Seventh
(crown): universal consciousness, mediumship [pituitary gland]

Sixth
(third eye): intuition, creative insight, clairvoyance [pineal gland]

Fifth
(throat): communication, clairaudience [thyroid gland, brain, eyes, ears, nose, mouth, bronchial tubes, esophagus]

Fourth
(heart): personal love and universal compassion [thymus, heart, lungs, shoulders]

Third
(solar): power, energy [adrenals, liver, gall bladder, stomach, blood and lymph]

Second
(sacral or splenic): emotions, security, clairsentience, [pancreas, kidneys, skin, uterus]

First
(root): grounding, survival [ovaries or testes (fertility), large intestine, bones]

LOCATION AND FUNCTION OF THE SEVEN MAIN CHAKRAS

D. Sedowsky '84

ment. Meanwhile the strong points of others don't threaten you or make you jealous. In fact, you're able to observe those who have skills you wish to emulate—physical skills from sewing to carpentry to acrobatics, mental skills such as mathematics and meditation, or any of the communication skills—and then start to practice them on your own.

When you work on your third chakra, begin by concentrating on your sense of self-worth. Self-worth gives rise to a sound and judicious use of personal power. In associating with spirit guides it's of utmost importance that you realize you have what it takes to remain in charge of the arrangement, otherwise you may fabricate so many paper demons that you'll have trouble cooperating with an actual companion.

The first, second and third chakras are often referred to as the lower chakras. They form the foundation of physical and emotional well-being—or the rickety underpinnings of illness, difficulty, and want. Since etiquette tells us to keep our lower bodies quite still, the vitality of our lower chakras and organs is apt to be inhibited, if not impaired. We're also likely to be ungrounded and easily upset. As the song says, "House built on a weak foundation: Will it stand? Oh, no!"

A good system of meditation promotes grounding. It serves to open and strengthen each chakra equally. You don't raise your awareness and achieve personal balance by neglecting or over-emphasizing any aspect of your being. In a balanced individual all seven major chakras are equal in size. People who concentrate exclusively on their higher development—who meditate for hours on their upper chakras and force themselves to eat ethereal diets when not fasting completely—are effectively discarding their God-given ability to keep their life together on a material plane. This is foolish and unnecessary.

You may have an extraordinary talent with some single chakra. You might wish to focus on one or two chakras that need work. But remember, only when all your centers are open and functioning in unison will you be traveling your true life path.

The **heart chakra** is the gateway between the lower and higher chakras. It is centered near the xiphoid process, the piece of cartilage at the base of the breastbone. The bodily functions associated with the fourth chakra are the pumping of the heart and the act of breathing.[4] Breathing comprises both the respiration of air and the circulation of essential life-force—also known as *prana, chi,* or *ruach* (the Hebrew

---

[4]There's an actual location behind the physical heart where the breathing impulse originates. By stimulating or calming the heart chakra, your breath rate can be quickened, slowed or made regular. Asthmatics and emphysemics, take note.

word translated biblically as "the Spirit of God" or simply "the Spirit").

Your fourth chakra has to do with the quality and extent of your joys and sorrows and the compassion you feel for your fellow beings. When your heart chakra is open and of adequate size, you're able to laugh and cry, sometimes simultaneously. Deep laughter and deep crying are both expressions of compassion.

The fourth also shapes your capacity to express and accept personal love, to demonstrate loving energy toward others and attract the same from them. With an open fourth, you appreciate life. You are able to experience oneness with the entirety of life, and you approach other people within the attitude that we're all equally fit for our individual purpose. Moreover, you have access to profound serenity, no matter what's going on outside yourself.

Blockage and/or constriction of the heart chakra causes tension throughout the whole body. Breathing gets shallow, as do the emotions. Signs of fourth-chakra trouble include a judgmental, know-it-all attitude, undependability, and a capacity for conditional love only ("If you do thus-and-so, then I'll love you").

We draw in love-energy through the upper middle back, between the fourth and sixth thoracic vertebrae. Having received this energy, we then mix it with our personal energy and radiate it, through the larger fourth-chakra opening in front, out to the world around us—plants, animals and human beings.

Shoulder pains on the right side, in back, indicate difficulty with accepting love; on the left, difficulty with giving it, or an emotional separation that has inflicted a deep wound. If the shoulder trouble is to the front, the situation is reversed: left-side aches or injuries indicate difficulty with receiving, and right-side problems denote difficulty with giving. Right-side problems may also point to a competitive nature that is being exercised incorrectly or excessively.

The thymus gland, key to the body's immune system, reflects the openness or the closed-off manner with which we meet the world on a fourth-chakra level. The thymus is pivotal in warding off cancer and in recovering from this disease.

Denying yourself the treats and joys of life and being stingy with others are two kinds of behavior that cause intense damage to the fourth chakra. Heart ailments represent an imbalance of some sort between the fourth and the first, through which we draw in the bounty of the world. When we habitually hoard this bounty—be it emotional, spiritual or material—instead of sharing it, we create a structure which inclines us to heart attacks, though what constitutes too much wealth is different for different people.

The first and fourth chakras are paired for good or ill. The capacity to be generous without giving up all that you have reveals a successful pairing, a balance between the inflow of your first and the outflow of your fourth. We're meant to draw abundance through the root chakra and send it out through the heart chakra. God is good to us, and so should we be to others.

Not all heart ailments are brought on by a lack of generosity. Children can develop heart problems because of feeling unloved by their families. Children are psychically and emotionally corded to one or both parents until late adolescence or early adulthood. The connection ensures their survival. When the cord is damaged or prematurely severed, this can precipitate a degenerative condition in the physical heart as well as an unloving behavior pattern. Once a negative fourth-chakra condition sets in, its nags at the person throughout life, arising again in each new stress situation which calls for a lot of heart-related energy.

Lies and half-truths also injure the fourth chakra, and especially the lungs. This is so whether you tell the lie yourself or accept it without challenge from someone else. The less lying you involve yourself in, the more your fourth opens, allowing you to be that much more truthful. And compassionate. Jesus' statement, "The truth shall set you free," is fourth-chakra wisdom. Asking for and providing the truth frees up the region of the heart and feels wonderful. You cherish yourself and feel like a lover. You feel *free* to be a lover—of God and neighbor, of life in general and spouse or special friend in particular.

When the heart chakra is embedded with untruth, or with fear of exposure and betrayal, this is the result of a false or pretentious self-image having ridden up from the first chakra, and it becomes very hard to generate feelings of love and intimacy. Since a relationship with a guide is profoundly intimate, it is vital that your first and fourth, and your sense of their connection, be well attended to. If you have a backlog of dishonesty, gradually relieve yourself of it by setting things straight with the people in your life. In any case, with a spirit companion there's really no hiding. Your guide knows what's on your mind before you verbalize it. So you have to be prepared to open yourself at least to the extent of semi-conditional love. Semi-conditional love describes a relationship in which each of you goes on loving the other, though every so often one of you incurs the other's stern displeasure or outright disapproval. Meanwhile, the fourth-chakra goal toward which your guide tries to lead you is unconditional love, which trusts in each person's ultimate enlightenment and knows that missteps and catastrophic detours are natural occurrences as one travels one's true path.

The **fifth chakra**, centered in the hollow of the throat, is your means of communicating with and ministering to the outside world. The functioning of most upper organs—brain, eyes, ears, mouth, nose, thyroid gland, bronchial tubes—is regulated by this chakra.

When the throat chakra is of healthy size and working well, all your senses are sharp. You think clearly and speak accurately and effectively. Your sincerity is obvious. You say exactly what you mean, and what you say is well-received. Your phrasing and tone are such that people are seldom put off or threatened or hurt by your words. You don't subvert your own intention in order to be polite, but neither do you inflict careless verbal injury. *Clairaudience*, the intuitive talent for hearing astral voices and music, is the psychic power that arises from the unencumbered activity of the throat chakra.

On the contrary, if you ignore what your senses are taking in, if you're apt to feel mortified over what you just said, if you have trouble asserting yourself verbally and articulating what you mean, if there's a big discrepancy between what you say and what you do, or if you tend to indulge in rumor and innuendo, it's the fifth chakra that needs attention. Another common pattern of fifth-chakra misuse is that of the authoritarian who is rigid of opinion, stiff-necked and tight-lipped in order to control the output of the mouth. As you work on restoring balance, strength and resilience to the fifth chakra, it helps enormously to suspend critical judgments and glimpse the spark of divinity in each person and in each facet of nature. This includes letting go of prejudices and vengeful schemes and refraining from loose, manipulative talk.

In most cases, your fifth closes down because you won't speak up. You don't trust the world with what you have to say, and you don't trust yourself to go ahead and say it. If such is the situation, strengthen your fifth by finding new outlets for your expressive energy. Let the radiance of your heart rise up and penetrate your throat. Or try humming so that the sound resonates throughout your neck.

Sound is the key to the opening of the fifth chakra. Crooning your children to sleep, chanting in a circle, and singing aloud are positive expressions of the primal scream. When your fifth is an open conduit, your speaking voice is clear and bell-like, without insinuating overtones. It conveys an appealing richness, and if you're musically inclined your abilities are vastly sharpened.

Like the first and fourth chakras, the second and fifth are paired up—more noticeably so in women and children. Owing to a fear of rejection, you may restrain yourself from speaking freely. In an effort to win acceptance, you may be heedlessly verbose and given to wild statements.

Inasmuch as the fifth chakra channels directly to every sense but touch, one of its main purposes is to keep you involved in the sensory world. Meanwhile your emotional life and sense of touch are nourished by the second chakra. In general, numbness is a two-level impairment that affects both the second and the fifth. When people shut off their hearing, fog their vision, or develop speech problems, it's often because they're allowing a pattern of emotional deadening to ride up from the sacral center to the throat center. Once a two-year-old girl was brought to me by her mother, who was afraid that the child was going deaf. After I worked with both parents to curtail their almost constant fighting and bickering, the girl's full hearing returned.

The third chakra also pairs with the fifth, particularly in men. When a man's self-worth is deficient, he lacks the guts to speak his mind. People who charge into a room or throw their weight around conversationally are showing third-fifth excess. Verbal battering is an extreme version of this.

The fifth pairs, in turn, with the seventh. In fact, good functioning of the fifth is crucial to the opening of the seventh. It's the first step on the path to clarity: the capacity to see through your pretensions, ambitions, errors and miseries by means of regular self-examination. With clarity, you have the advantage of common sense, whether or not you happen to be intellectually gifted in other ways. You don't waste your energy on dragons of your own making.

Unfortunately, the fifth can also be the center from which you spin worry, which is the opposite of clarity. Worry stems from deluded sense perceptions, fed by second-chakra insecurity. Most worries dissolve in the light of self-knowledge and self-acceptance, aided by the self-assurance that results from the day-to-day discipline of working toward these goals. When you find yourself worrying about someone else, look to see what aspect of yourself might be at the root of your anxiety.

If you're agitated within, it's next to impossible to receive a precise reading of any message your spirit helper may be trying to convey. Even straight, loud talk can't get through to your conscious mind. The clarity of an open fifth chakra is what gives you an ear for inner wisdom and understanding.

The **sixth chakra**, the *third eye*, is the dwelling place of the soul or inner being. It is centered in the front part of the cranium, behind the brow and between the physical eyes. Its opening at the back is just above the atlas vertebra, the topmost vertebra in the neck. Unlike the lower five chakras, the sixth does not connect directly with the body's organs. It does relate, however, to the activity of the pineal gland and the health of the mind, as distinct from the brain. It also ties in with the first and fourth chakras, and either benefits or suffers as a consequence.

The sixth chakra is your line to creative energy, and to the kind of comprehension that transcends intellectual knowing. Its two principal functions are intuition and inspiration—access to knowledge that is not learned externally, hunches and visions beyond the reach of the five senses. The sixth is therefore the main channel for all the creative arts. Though sixth-chakra impressions are primarily pictorial, the sixth also acts in combination with the other chakras to turn concepts into worldly reality. The sixth and fifth, working together, enable you to hear original melodies and songs, in addition to details of songs remembered. When you dance with an open sixth, you *are* the dance —creativity in physical motion. The energy just pours through you.

Since the sixth chakra is the organ of subliminal vision, the way to "see" your spirit guide is through the third eye. When the sixth is open and balanced, *clairvoyance* results. Those who wish their psychic and creative abilities to expand are advised to work slowly and lovingly at opening the sixth for themselves. On the other hand, consistent failure to honor one's intuitions inevitably causes a shrinking of the sixth.

Blockage of the sixth chakra can lead to an ultra-rational attitude, or, in combination with a restricted first, to a diminished and negative self-image. Hallucinations and spiritual exhibitionism are symptoms of imbalance. Excess is personified by the God-playing guru, or by the kind of person who is both intensely overbearing and psychically sapping. In our culture, people routinely fog up and impair their sixth-chakra envisioning by steady use of alcohol and/or processed tobacco.

It's very difficult to keep in touch with a guide unless you remain clear and receptive in your sixth chakra. Almost all the messages you send and receive are interpreted through the sixth. So it's of utmost importance that you develop it and protect it, using the techniques outlined in the next chapter. Then you'll be able to open up your third eye with full confidence that you won't be invaded or hurt.

With respect to spirit-guide work and your general well-being, it isn't necessary that you have perfect balance in the sixth chakra, or in any of the chakras. Certainly you'll want to keep advancing toward this end, but in the meantime perfection is not a prerequisite. You are encouraged to utilize the powers of the sixth chakra to the best of your capacity.

The **seventh chakra,** the *crown chakra,* is centered at the widest spot of the fontanelle that you had as a baby. Associated with the pituitary gland, the seventh is your instrument of direct communication with the divine light. This communication stimulates your evolution toward at-one-ment with the Creator and all of Creation.

At first, access to this at-one-ment is temporary. But it grows more and more lasting as your seventh chakra becomes more open, clear and active. Your consciousness becomes such that you comprehend the variety and complexity as well as the connectedness of all things. You are in wakeful contact with each plane of your existence, and have the integrity and courage to deeply examine each of your inner worlds. Your visionary insight, strong and incisive, gives you a thorough understanding of maps of the universe, such as cosmology and astrology. Your personality is also very strong, yet gentle. You're able to manage earthly elements and to flow with forces beyond our earth, yet you do so with ample kindness for humanity. Meanwhile you maintain a rather detached perspective on yourself and your many little ways. At the time of your death you remain totally aware, knowing that you are dying and going ahead with it anyhow.

The evolved consciousness of an open crown chakra, together with good function and balance in the other major centers, may be called self-realization. Self-realization does not come about unless all the chakras are equally active. A four-year-old child may have a wide-open seventh, but rarely will he be able to help you make an apple pie or even tie his own shoes. There are also adults, some of them creative geniuses, whose seventh, sixth, and fifth are their only fully functional chakras and who consequently require someone else to look after them and care for their worldly needs.

When your seventh is closed, you create or perpetuate a condition of limited growth. In some cultures, men and women alike wear head coverings that tend to restrict seventh-chakra activity and curtail personal unfolding. To keep on living a limited life is the most severe form of inner dishonesty and delusion. For many people the only experience of access to the Source occurs at the moment of death.

A closed seventh leads both to a fear of dying and a fear of enjoying life. The delusion takes hold that if you really enjoy life, you're bound to lose it. So you cling to the closed-box attitude that "life is suffering, and then you're dead."

Few of us are clear in the seventh chakra. For some of us, it's enough merely to be aware of the fact that we *have* a seventh chakra. To take the first steps toward opening and using the seventh calls for great courage and dedication, because there's no turning back. Once you begin the process, you'll never again rest content with devoting yourself to conventional goals for their own sake. No degree of wealth or status or worldly achievement will seem sufficient, unless you can manage this while realizing your seventh-chakra perceptions and priorities.

In taking LSD and other hallucinogens, the flower children deliberately or inadvertently got a taste of how an open seventh feels. As a result they began to criticize and reject several ingredients in the cultural recipe for success. For some, this led to a fuller life. Others, less grounded or less capable of bridging the gap between daily life and an alternate reality, became addicted to a critical form of expression and/or to further drugs.

It's far preferable, of course, to open the seventh very gradually, by the natural means of meditation and prayer. As you do so, meanness and selfish ambition will melt away. You'll find it increasingly difficult to act "unconsciously" or "with diminished capacity," above all toward another person. This doesn't mean that you refrain from anger and other strong emotions. It means that you are able to use anger appropriately and constructively, as a tool for self-defense or for sparking another person's higher self.

When you start living your life according to seventh-chakra consciousness, you enter into the realm of unconditional love—within yourself, with other human beings, in relation to the spirit guides with whom you cooperate, and in relation to God. Unconditional love is the greatest power in the universe. It burns your negative karma like so much dry tinder, and can enable you to do ten years' growing in a fraction of that time.

Effects of fear and bliss. Each of your chakras contains a degree of fear. But the crippling effects of fear permeate some chakras more tellingly than others, depending upon the way you live. We each have patterns of behavior and expression (or non-expression) that we are working in, on, and through. By reviewing the patterns of action and reaction that get you in trouble, by noting central body areas that feel painful or cold or insensitive to touch, and by observing your recurrent ailments and the parts affected, you can deduce for yourself which chakras need primary attention.

People hang on to their fears for two reasons. First, because of habit. Second, because fear acts as a stimulant. When you're physically exhausted, or emotionally frazzled by a no-growth routine, the shots of adrenaline from your old familiar fear can stir up an artificial high to keep you going.

In a state of bliss your chakras are free from anxiety. Bliss might be described as a capacity for dancing on the flat of the sword rather than along its edge. This is different from the "bliss" claimed by certain religious fanatics who exude a sort of smiling hysteria, although their fears are evidenced by the need to ballyhoo their own transcendence and act superior. When you're in a true state of bliss, you brim with the desire to help others along, but you have no stake in turning them into faithful devotees or replicas of yourself. You realize that if others are to encounter bliss, they must follow their own inner light, no matter how brightly your light shines forth.

The experience of loving someone else, especially over a period of years, through good times and bad, is a form of bliss. Having learned to accept the other person as he or she is, you generate a measure of divine radiance. A long-term, caring relationship with a guide can bring you to the same enlightened condition.

Effects of grief. Grief comes about when you feel rejected and powerless, or when you suffer an intimate loss that you can do nothing about. It therefore involves an incapacitating interplay among the first four chakras. A person in mourning undergoes a nonlinear onslaught of five distinct emotional states: denial, anger, rationalization, depression and acceptance. Like fear, a full expression of grief affects the entire consciousness.

Unlike fear, however, grief doesn't interfere with a guide's efforts to reach you. Fear shrinks you down and armors you over. But in the midst of grief, communication with a spirit companion becomes easier because you are feeling laid-open and needy, both emotionally and spiritually. Many people have reported that their only contact with a guide (or guides) occurred at some deeply grievous moment—perhaps following a divorce, or in connection with a death in the family. One purpose of this book is to provide information and encouragement for expanding a crisis-contact into a permanent partnership with a spirit helper.

3
GROUNDING
AND MEDITATION

Grounding

When interacting with a guide or ally, you need to know who *you* are, so that the two of you don't merge to an undesirable degree. It's best to relate to your guide from a standpoint of confidence, self-focus and self-love. Then, no matter what happens, you can absorb the experience or reject it with an attitude of comparative security. The key to minimizing your fears is to be well-grounded, with a clear aura and unobstructed chakras.

Grounding is contact with the earth, a condition of being centered in your earthly self, a sense of stability and inner peace that pervades you on multiple levels of awareness: physically, emotionally, mentally, intuitively and spiritually. We are meant, during our bodily sojourn, to ride between heaven and earth, to be neither so excessively earthy that we bog down and stagnate nor so lofty that we lose touch with everyday life.

Grounding has a temporal aspect as well as spatial qualities. When you're well-grounded, you live primarily in the present. You have an eye to both the future and the past, but you're not concentrated on either one to the exclusion of life here and now.

If you are grounded at the moment of receiving what would ordinarily be an upsetting phone call, your reaction tends to be resilient, calm and resourceful. If you're grounded when someone offers you an interesting bit of information, the information doesn't slip through your consciousness or go bouncing around in your head; it finds its proper context. Mystic and spiritual experiences also have a more profound effect on you if you're centered when they occur, and your memory of them remains clearer.

Usually grounding is subconscious, and so is the lack of it. However, grounding may be cultivated consciously as a technique for staying centered within yourself, so that you don't take on the unwanted vibrations of other individuals, places or situations. When you learn to ground yourself well, you can go on being sensitive to prevailing conditions and people's intentions, but you're less caught up in these outside influences and they make a less disturbing impression upon you. In a crisis you're able to be responsibly involved without getting swept off your feet. You maintain your integrity and sense of proportion.

In addition to emotional stability, the rewards of good grounding include refined attunement to yourself and others, accurate body awareness as you move around, appreciation for the overall well-being of your physical form, and alleviation of your customary aches and pains. If you practice staying as grounded as you can over a period of years, you're apt to treat yourself and the people who come into your life with warmth and humor.

When your grounding is not good, your spatial understanding is impaired. You tend to stumble into things and you may take frequent spills. You're liable to turn an ankle or wrench a knee. You might have trouble with your hip joints, or with persistent black and blue marks. Moreover, you seem to have a hard time holding your ground, both physically and emotionally. A tight situation knocks you off-center. You have difficulty recognizing and demonstrating your deepest feelings, and you may blurt out foolish or revealing statements that you later regret.

Good grounding is essential to the proper functioning of your mental body as well as your physical body. To contact a guide, you have to be able to trust yourself mentally. In addition to balancing and stabilizing you, grounding and meditation are means for bringing about mental flow as well as peace of mind, and for ensuring the continuance of both. The result is that you learn better and you're much more likely to enjoy the experiences you have.

Grounding Techniques

If you suffer from periodic weakness of will or find yourself overly influenced by other people's energies, you'll discover that techniques for grounding and meditation are especially helpful in strengthening your stance. With regular practice, you gradually come to know your innermost self with clarity and to assert your desires with force.

In recent years, various exercises have been developed which improve physical grounding. Exercises taught by advocates of bioenergetic and/or Reichian body work involve deep abdominal breathing (through the mouth, with the jaw slack) coordinated with positions and moves that promote the release of tension—primarily in the feet, ankles, knees, and pelvic region.

Running and sports that involve continual, nonviolent activity have a grounding effect. There are also traditional means specifically designed for creating a grounded state. One of these is hatha yoga; another is correct meditation. Some teachers of meditative techniques emphasize attention to the upper body only, but during meditation your first chakra and your entire perineal area should be as receptive and relaxed as your mouth and jaw. Both openings need to sense the ebb and flow of the cleansing breaths. When you get up and walk around after meditating, you should have as much awareness and tactile sensitivity with the soles of your feet as with your eyes and hands.

Before you start to meditate—and especially if you're new to meditation—it's important that you have something light to eat. Eating is an automatic grounding technique, both because it's mainly a physical experience and because food is of the earth. After you've been meditating for some time, you won't require anything other than inner suggestion to ground yourself.

If you have a tendency to drift off into space when you close your eyes in meditation, and if it's a warm season of the year, you might go outdoors and sit against a tree or lie down on the ground. Plants facilitate grounding—trees, in particular. When feeling frightened, you can hug a tree, and many times the fright will dissipate.

Everybody knows of a geographical place with which they resonate, where they feel buoyant and at ease. For some people, it's the seashore. Others are at their best in the high mountains or out in the desert. It is of obvious benefit to your grounding ability and your overall well-being if you're in love with where you live.

To further strengthen your grounding prior to meditation and spirit-guide work, concentrate on the chakras in the arches of your feet. (Although there are actually two chakras per arch, we'll consider them as one.) Now, from each foot chakra, send a grounding rod 80 feet down through grass, dust, and mantle, and into the rock deep beneath. Picture yourself doing this and take note of the sensations that result. The grounding rods firm up your earthly connections so that you don't float away when you shut your eyes and open your mind.

Make your grounding rods out of a substance that appeals to you. You may end up with brass cylinders, terra cotta pipes, telephone poles, or sturdy saplings with roots at the lower extremity to grab the bedrock.

Grounding rods are not material extensions of your feet. At first they're products of your imagination. As time goes on, however, you'll begin to feel them physically, nursing and pulling gently at your arches, helping you ride in balance between earth and cosmos. Even if you have difficulty picturing things, do your best to attempt the visualization. As long as you keep trying, you'll begin to feel them and finally to see them.

Grounding yourself in an airplane or above the fourth story of a building poses more of a problem, but it's not impossible. As discussed in Chapter 1, the reality we inhabit is a product of community imagination, based on a belief system in which we have been carefully tutored since infancy. It doesn't matter what floor you live on. Whether you're 40 stories up or cruising at 40,000 feet, just think of yourself at street level when you activate your grounding apparatus.

Meditation

Before attempting contact with your guide, you are strongly advised to do the following meditative exercise. Working with guides can sometimes throw you off-balance. As a result, the meditation presented here has been designed to ground you in your physical/emotional self and to center you in your higher self, so that when you bring in your guide you'll be settled down but wide awake.

Choose a meditative position that feels comfortable and relaxing. Two positions deserve special recommendation:

(1) Lying down on a bed or some form of padding—something that isn't too thick or soft, preferably made of natural materials (polyurethane foam may be convenient, but it isn't natural). Lie on your back with your knees drawn up and the soles of your feet flat on the padding, floor, or ground. The horizontal position is best for beginners because it grounds all the major chakras.

(2) Sitting tailor-fashion, perhaps on a cushion or low stool, with your legs folded but uncrossed. Your spine should be comfortably straight, neither curved nor tilted. A vertical posture opens you to higher levels of experience. If you have trouble with stiffness in your knees and ankles, you can also meditate while seated in a straight-backed chair.

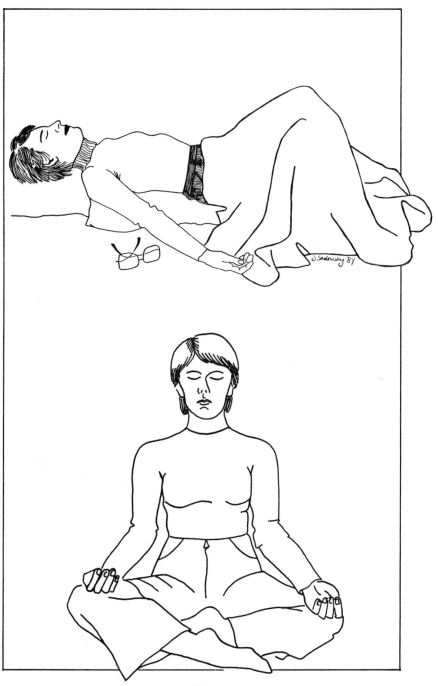

Remove eyeglasses and contact lenses; these interfere with meditation. Hearing aids should also be removed. Most times they start to buzz as you proceed with the exercise, due to changes of wavelength in the brain's vibrations.

When the ambient temperature is less than 80 °F (27 °C), cover yourself. Body activity slows down during meditation, and you'll want to keep warm so that bodily discomfort doesn't distract you from what you're concentrating on mentally. Be particularly careful to keep feet and legs warm, otherwise cramping may occur.

Close your physical eyes, and in your mind's eye visualize the grounding rods emerging from your feet at the arches and sinking effortlessly toward the center of the earth, 80 feet down (25 meters). From your first chakra, put down one more grounding rod, to stabilize you like the third leg of a tripod.

Now start to take slow, complete breaths—in and out, very relaxed. If possible, breathe through your nose. As you bring air into your lungs, bring energy up through your feet into your first chakra. Then, as you exhale, direct the energy up along your spinal column and out the top of your head. With each in-breath you bring up earth energy, which grounds you. With each out-breath, you move this earth energy up the length of your spinal column so that it passes through the major chakras and helps clear them of psychic and emotional debris. By breathing well and directing an upward flow of energy, you alleviate your burdens of the day, and the upsetting factors in your life begin to shrink down to manageable proportions.

When you breathe, let the physical breaths reach into your abdomen, your intestines, the muscles of your back, the sides of your chest, your breastbone and collarbone and shoulders. Let them fill your entire neck. Merely to expand your chest is an erroneous notion of what constitutes proper breathing. As you inhale, let your abdomen fill first, then your chest. When you exhale, empty your chest and then your abdomen. This is one of the breathing methods used by yogis and other enlightened masters to nurture their consciousness beyond the five senses.

Breathing deeply and abdominally is how you generally breathe when you're asleep. Even if you've learned to limit your breathing while awake, you can't constrain yourself so effectively when sleeping. Your waking body may have become so rigid over the years that you are unable to take full breaths without effort. If so, meditative breathing will help you loosen up restrictive muscle patterns in the abdomen, chest and shoulders. It will stimulate your digestion of both food and experience. By practicing a form of breathing that maximizes your physical involvement, you improve your emotional flexibility and overall health.

When you feel at ease with full, rhythmic respiration, add one more element as a further cleansing agent and neutralizer of your negativity. Together with each in-breath, start to bring a vibrant green color up through your grounding rods, feet, and legs, and draw it into your first chakra. Then, as you exhale, move the green light up along your spinal column and out the top of your head. Take at least twenty breaths in this manner, incorporating the flow of color into your respiratory rhythm.

Now, through the crown chakra at the top of your head, begin to breathe in an energy the color of gold, a cosmic energy to complement the green earth energy and invoke a balance between the universal and the physical. Pull the golden color down along your spinal column through the first chakra and into your legs. Then exhale it out your feet and through the grounding rods, down into the earth. Fill yourself with the gold, just as you did with the green. Repeat this at least four times.

At this point start combining the two energy breaths. Inhale golden energy down through your crown and green energy up through your grounding rods. Draw it all into your first chakra, at the base of your spine just under the tailbone. There the energies mix, becoming golden-green in hue. Now exhale the golden-green color along your spinal column and out the top of your head. Repeat this process of drawing in, mixing, and exhaling for at least sixteen breaths.

You are now adequately grounded and ready to commence a more thorough and intensive chakra cleaning.

Continuing to take slow, full breaths, visualize your first chakra and fill it with golden-green light. Keep opening and filling the chakra until it measures three inches in diameter. With all your chakras, a three-inch diameter is the optimal size for maintenance of a healthy, balanced life.

When you bring a color into a chakra during meditation, picture it and feel it as an astral beam or a ray of light that you're pulling into your body, perpendicular to the up-and-down axis of your main energy flow. Draw the beam into the chakra's larger opening (in front, except for the first chakra) and let it filter out through the chakra's smaller opening, so that the flow of universal energy continues its circulation, introducing lighted freshness and removing whatever you're ready to give up from your body and auric field.

As you inspect your first chakra's condition, you may perceive grey spots or some of the other negative shades listed in the preceding chapter. There may be a sensation of physical tension or bloatedness. Perhaps you experience recall of an event that occurred long ago, in particular an event relating to some aspect of your basic survival needs. If your perceptions and/or memories are unpleasant, get out an imaginary vacuum cleaner and vacuum them up, so that just the clear golden-green remains. As soon as the chakra is thoroughly cleaned out and permeated with healthy color, replace the golden-green with a bright yellow. In Chinese medicine, yellow is considered the color of the earth. It's also the color of the sun, which sustains all earthly life.

Now, leaving the bright yellow in your first chakra, exhale four times in moderately rapid succession to clear the passageway that connects the first and second chakras. (The compensatory in-breaths occur automatically.) If the passageway still feels impeded, repeat the four out-breaths.

At this point visualize your second chakra, centered two inches below your navel. Once again, go through the process of purifying with golden-green light and vacuuming up any contents that don't belong there. The second is your emotional center, and it's one of the hardest chakras to keep clean. Sometimes it's so difficult to let go of a stagnant worry or fear that it helps to picture the situation that triggers the emotion and wire this picture to a stick of dynamite which you then blow up. Using imaginary dynamite is not damaging to you or anyone else; nor is it depleting, because immediately following the explosion you fill the chakra with fresh golden-green energy.

If blasting with dynamite seems too crude or violent, put the undesired material into a basket attached to a helium-filled balloon. Then send the balloon out over the ocean. When it's far enough offshore, invite a little bird to fly past and give it a peck.[1]

The color appropriate to the second chakra is a bright medium blue. After cleaning the second with yellow-green, bathe it in bright blue light. Blue has long been associated with water and the emotions. It sustains confidence and emotional flexibility.

After four more panting out-breaths to clear the passageway between the second and third chakras, move your awareness up to the third, two inches above the navel, and repeat the cleansing process. The third chakra is your power center. Its element is fire. Once you've cleaned it, fill it with a golden-orange or pumpkin-orange light.

---

[1]You might also try using cleansers that are in keeping with the energetic focus of each chakra. For the first: sand. For the second: soap and water. For the third: a purifying fire. For the fourth: the vacuum cleaner. For the fifth: music, or possibly the smoke from burning cedar needles, sage leaf, angelica root or sweet grass.

Should you ever feel powerless, either in a specific situation or over a period of time, you can boost your third chakra protection by imaging a brass oriental-style firescreen in front of your upper abdominal area. An astral beam of golden orange will also help.

Exhale eight times, to sweep out the passage between the third and fourth chakras. The fourth, centered near the xiphoid process at the base of your sternum, is the first of the higher chakras. Its element is air. Clean it with a plain yellow-gold color rather than with greenish gold. As you do your cleaning, a dread of intimacy may arise—or a welling-up of sorrow, a burst of joy, an urge to laugh or cry. These are feelings that have come up to be expressed and released. Experience them thoroughly, but with a degree of detachment. Observe them as they wash through you, fill you, and then drain away.

The color with which you imbue your heart chakra depends upon your present need. If the physical heart is weak, strengthen it with gold. If you need to show more love toward your fellow beings, a bright green is the light to bring in. Should you be having difficulty with personal love—either in forming close associations or maintaining them peacefully—then pink is the color to place in the fourth chakra. Pink and rose-pink energy are valuable tools for stimulating expression of all aspects of love and compassion in your life.[2]

Now do sixteen short out-breaths; the passageway that joins the fourth and fifth is the longest connector between chakras. The fifth chakra, located in the hollow of the throat, is associated with the element ether. It should be cleaned with gold and strengthened with turquoise blue. If, during the cleaning, you recall situations wherein you wish you had spoken and did not, say the desired words in your head right now. Speaking your feelings, even to yourself—or aloud, to the walls of the room—releases communicative energy that has been trapped in your throat chakra.

---

[2]Another excellent method for cleaning the fourth chakra is the *amitabha* breath, a technique which involves you with another person, perhaps someone with whom you are presently having a hard time. Sit facing each other, about eighteen inches apart. (You can also *imagine* that you are sitting and facing the other person.) Now start to breathe slowly and regularly, each at your own pace. As you breathe in, visualize the out-breath of your partner (or adversary) coming toward you in a gentle S-curve that enters the lower part of your heart chakra. As you breathe out, the energy of your exhale curves up and out of the upper portion of your heart chakra, and then back down to form a figure eight as it enters your partner's heart chakra from below.

It's easier to follow the path of the amitabha breath if one of you uses the right forefinger to trace the figure eight in the space between you. This tracing action, the visualization of the energy flow, and the gradual pacing of your breath will move the two of you into a much-improved rapport.

Many times blockages in the fifth are ride-ups from the fourth. Should your fifth continue to feel blocked or cluttered after cleaning it with gold and filling it with turquoise, go back and repeat your work on the fourth so that the heart material doesn't keep welling up so intensely. You might also penetrate the fourth with a pink beam of light. As indicated above, pink and rose-pink facilitate the release of loving energy, and this in turn allows the fifth to operate more freely.

Exhale eight times and concentrate on the sixth chakra, just above and behind the eyes. As you clean it with gold, let your intuition flow unrestrained. All manner of images may come forward at this time. Just let them pass in review; anything you can make use of will come back to you later.

In case a distressing image persists and doesn't fade, make a package of its contents. If it originated as part of an interaction with somebody else, picture the person and hand over the package. Forgivingly, graciously, say that you don't want it any more. If you don't know where the material comes from, simply give it back to God to be reabsorbed.

When your sixth feels clear, fill it with one of three colors: magenta, blue-white or bright gold. Magenta fortifies your intuitive power, blue-white enhances purity of thought and gold furthers contact with unconditional love.

After four more out-breaths, clean the seventh or crown chakra with gold light and fill it with bright blue-purple. If your seventh feels particularly murky, it's probably clouded with old images of what spiritual life is really about. Release these images as you cleanse it with the gold. Permeating the seventh with blue-purple will not only clarify the spiritual activity that is correct for you but will help you become more familiar with the inner planes of consciousness, and braver about moving around between them.[3]

Having finished with the cleaning of your chakras, turn your attention to the condition of your aura. Your purpose is to manifest an aura that has no holes, tears or discolorations. To this end, picture a golden egg suspended in the air a few feet in front of your midsection. The egg begins to expand at a rapid rate. It becomes as big as an ostrich egg, then as big as a football. Soon it's even larger than you are, four feet larger in all directions. Now, in your mind's eye, step right into the middle of this huge golden egg.[4] This envelops you in the protection of the strongest color in the universe.

You're cleansed and grounded, open and balanced—ready here and now to meet up with anything or anyone.

Variations on the above meditative procedure may be in order after you've been doing it for a while. If you're prone to misuse your power, for instance, you may wish to tone it down by bathing your third chakra in a bright green color rather than with the pumpkin-orange. The green light neutralizes and heals. If your throat chakra is constricted due to a physical ailment or an emotional condition, you might suffuse it with an amethyst color instead of the turquoise. Later on, when you and your guide have become acquainted, the guide will sometimes suggest that you use a certain color in a certain chakra. Consult the color list in Chapter 2 to see what energy is being prescribed.

A good rule of thumb is that chakras one through four may be filled with green at any time, and chakras four through seven may be filled with gold—a reliable recourse in case you forget which color goes where. It is recommended, however, that you do the meditation exactly as outlined, permeating each chakra with the designated color. This meditation has been used extensively by large and small groups,

---

[3]Opening the seventh chakra often brings up fears of dying, because many people open this chakra only at the time of death.

[4]In the hours subsequent to meditation, your own natural colors will gradually return, somewhat purified. Meanwhile the shape of your aura will recreate itself along the complete lines of the golden ovoid.

and has proved highly effective in enabling people to center themselves. It is also often successful in bringing together seeker and guide. Meditation simultaneously calms you down, uplifts you, and sharpens your awareness, so that discarnate teachers can come through to you with the messages they convey.

4
MEETING YOUR GUIDE

You have learned about your major chakras and about your auric field, and you now have a potent system of meditation to clean out your chakras, heal your aura, and thoroughly ground yourself. The meditative self-cleansing and the grounding practice prepare you to meet your guide without physical stress, mental confusion, emotional anguish or spiritual alarm. To ground yourself still further, eat a small portion of your favorite food. When I give day-long classes in spirit-guide work I always have the participants share a midday meal, to be sure they have grounded themselves.

If you have not done the meditation or if you have been fasting, you have no business attempting to meet your guide for the first time. If you go ahead without proper preparation, you do so contrary to the authors' advice.

When you meet your guide, you should be in a suitable place, one that helps you to feel relaxed and centered. The optimal location for you may be indoors or outdoors. You may know it from past experience or set out to discover it by trial and error. You might travel to Mt. Shasta or Mt. Katahdin, or any other area which, according to native tradition, is endowed with the right vibratory field for spiritual work. Some people find water to be a special comfort, and they go to the beach or look for a place beside a creek or a river. If in doubt, seek out pleasant surroundings with which you're familiar.

Perhaps you have found the right general area but are still unsure of precisely your best spot. If so, walk around the area for a while, your head empty of thoughts. Even prior to contact, your guide is often able to provide assistance. After all, on the level of intention the communication between the two of you has already begun. Your guides are looking forward to the relationship at least as much as you are. They want to help you get through to them, and you can take advantage of this by letting them turn you in just the right direction and lead you to the perfect spot. If at home, you might end up in your favorite chair or somewhere out in the garden. On the other hand, you may be impelled to move the household furniture around in order to clear a particular space. In the opening chapter of *The Teachings of Don Juan*, Carlos Castaneda gives a detailed account of what he went through in his initial efforts to locate his *sitio*.

Two of the best positions for your body are the two meditative positions previously recommended: either lying on your back with your knees drawn up and your feet flat on the floor, or seated tailor-fashion on a cushion. Whatever position you choose to begin with, should your body feel wrongly aligned or start to get uncomfortable, adjust yourself accordingly. Physical discomforts and distractions will impede your progress and may even prevent you from making spirit contact.

Your eyes are closed, your body and mind refreshed by the meditation. At this point don't be surprised if you feel yourself start to spin, counterclockwise, at a slow to moderate speed. This is the so-called cosmic spin, and there's no need to be frightened or to stop yourself. Another thing: If your legs begin to shake, or if your body begins to quiver all over, recognize that these are natural releases, sometimes referred to as *kriyas*. Kriyas include such varied events as a letting-go of fear or an uprush of energy through the first chakra. Leg kriyas are common because they indicate that you're in the process of grounding yourself more emphatically. (Women in childbirth almost always have leg kriyas.) Some people are moved to hum or to make other sounds. Some start to laugh or cry.

As long as you have meditated adequately, you may have no kriyas at all. You needn't feel that something is missing if they fail to occur. But if they do occur, there's no cause for concern. Whatever happens, try to experience it as an expression of *your* energy. Feel how this energy moves you, and then begin to encourage its gradual upward passage along your spinal column and out the top of your head.

Now ground again and ask your guide to come forward. This may take some concentrated quiet time. Though guides can arrive instantaneously, not all contacts occur right away. If you wish, phrase your request in the form of an affirmation: "I, (name), am ready, able, and open to receive my life guide on the conscious plane."

It may not seem plausible that such simple steps can enable you to contact your guide. It might seem much more reasonable that spirit contacts are the result of months or even years of preparation. This is not so, however. Your guide is always in readiness. People in my classes are frequently astonished at how easy spirit communication can be.

At the moment of making contact, it's very important that you be filled with compassion, both for the spirit entity and for yourself. Compassion is the ability nonjudgmentally to accept and bear with personal reality, another's or one's own. Without compassion you may end up deluding yourself, projecting a positive or negative image from your ego. Contact and communication suffer unless you let your spirit friends behave as individuals. By imposing too many expectations, you disturb your guides' natural warmth and good intentions. You also saddle them with the added task of either transcending your image demands or reshaping their presence along acceptable lines. It's even possible for you to cause them the equivalent of emotional pain. Therefore, whenever summoning up a spirit helper, send them a ray of compassion direct from the heart chakra.

How will you experience your guide's response? Will it be through your ordinary senses? Oftentimes, yes. You may see your guide, either with your eyes closed or with them open, depending on your skill—though it's advisable to keep your eyes closed until you're so familiar with the visual impression that you start to anticipate its details. You may hear your guide: your name spoken aloud, a line of song, a distinctive vocabulary and style of delivery. You may notice a characteristic scent, a whiff of tobacco or perfume, or perhaps a more subtle aromatic tone. You may feel a certain presence, much as you sense the vibration of someone coming up behind you. Or you may have an intuitive perception similar to that of entering a crowded room and knowing that somebody you love is in there somewhere.

Although there are spirit helpers who, never having taken physical form, are without sex, most of them are distinctly male or female. Remember, however, that how you perceive your guide is a product of the translating procedure described in *Edgar Cayce Returns*, by Leichtman and Johnson (Ariel Press, Columbus, Ohio, 1978). "We actually appear rather like a ball of light or energy. But there's a translating mechanism in the psychic's or medium's head that puts arms and legs and a face and clothing on the image. Of course, we stimulate this kind of impression when we make contact with the psychic or medium because it's easier for a psychic to deal with a spook[1] who looks somewhat human. It's also easier for the psychic to maintain contact if the spook keeps more or less in the character of one of his or her physical incarnations."

However you become aware of the presence in your vicinity, rest assured that this is, indeed, a guide of yours. Begin by asking for a name. The name you get first is the correct one, even if it sounds like nothing you ever heard before.[2] Sometimes you'll get several names in sequence. There may be several guides trying to contact you, but more likely it's just one guide in the process of switching visual image and name in an effort to appeal to you. As long as the energetic quality of the presence continues to feel roughly the same, and as long as the presence stays in the same place relative to your body—say, above your left shoulder—then you can safely conclude that it's one and the same guide.

If there seem to be diverse presences approaching you from several different directions, there may actually be different guides trying to get through. Should you be blessed with more than one guide, they'll all want to be known by you while you're in a receptive state. Later in the day you might do a second session and call in someone else. But it's less confusing and less threatening to get to know your guides one at a time. Usually they're sensitive to this, and the others will wait patiently in the background until you have met and made acquaintance with your life guide (an encounter which poses minimal difficulty, inasmuch as you're already accustomed to your life guide's energy, having felt it around you since infancy).

If confronted with two guides vying for your attention, be very firm. Tell one of them to hold off a few minutes while you get to know the name and purpose of the other. It's impossible to open up to two guides at once with equal concentration—just as impossible as it is to talk on the phone with two strangers at the same time and come away with a clear sense of what each one is really like.

After ascertaining your guide's name, always try to find out why he or she is there. Ask him what purpose he might have in interacting with you. Ask her what she might expect of you in the way of personal learning. It may be that your guide is not able to furnish a full explan-

[1]Guides like to be called "spooks" as a term of endearment.

[2]It may be a name that the guide goes by in the world of spirit. Sometimes it's a generic name, relating to the guide's Source Self or Oversoul, as distinct from that of an individual. But it's much more likely that you'll meet your guide in his form as George the Iowa farmer boy who knew you from a lifetime when you were a young Iowa Indian and who, despite his fascination with you, chased you off his father's land.

nation at the outset. But even when the explanation is direct and not in the least cryptic, you may still resist its significance, since it often pertains to an area of understanding or a quality of behavior in which you're lacking.

Some people have difficulty meeting any guide, their life guide included. In the classes I give, it's not uncommon for all participants to make discernible contact. But just as frequently there are one or more people who report, "Nothing happened."

Even if you *want* to meet your guide, you may have an underlying opposition to realizing this contact. Should you suspect that such is the case, set aside a good chunk of time alone and look deep into yourself. Ask yourself if you're honestly ready to accept the reality of a spirit-human partnership and the two-world view that this kind of partnership emphasizes. Often the block to acceptance is the voice of an authority whose view is confined to the material world only. The voice chides, mocks, threatens, belittles. But you can acknowledge the one-sided opinion and let it go. Clean it out of each of your chakras and fill your aura with the willingness and readiness to extend your sense limits. Prepare yourself thoroughly, perhaps over a period of time; then try again to make contact with your guide.

If your resistance is extreme, see Chapter 10, "Borrowing and Lending Guides." And keep working on broadening your viewpoint to comfortably embrace the world of spirit.

Months may go by before you can begin to appreciate the benefits of your new partner. Chapter 6 is designed to assist you in learning to converse and cooperate with your guide, while Chapter 12 focuses on accurate interpretation of the visual and aural stimuli your guide transmits.

Once in a private session I was coaching the owner of a new restaurant, a woman named Francesca. Francesca was agitated over the financial prospects of her enterprise, and she had been seeking advice from every source. She came to me in an effort to consult with her spirit guides. As it turned out, she contacted two of them: Harry, a former accountant, and a character who called himself Timothy. Later that same day Harry supplied Francesca with some sound dollars-and-cents counsel which contributed to the subsequent success of her business. She was delighted. But seven or eight months further on, she stopped by to tell me that Harry was around rather infrequently, and now her main guide was Timothy. It appeared that Timothy's special talent was to encourage laughter. By this time I knew Francesca a bit better, and I could recognize how appropriate it was for Timothy to have assumed such importance in her life. She was a workaholic, and one good antidote for her overwork was a strong relationship with a guide who liked to go out and have fun. As so often happens, she reached out and received what she needed as well as what she requested.

Sometimes guides like to provoke you, but it's a breach of universal law for them to frighten you. For beings on the discarnate planes it is an axiom that human beings are to be respected and dealt with very carefully, inasmuch as physical form is so delicate. No guide is allowed to scare you intentionally. If severely frightened, you might suffer mental or bodily damage, or even lose control of your life. In any case you would tend to avoid further communication.

On the contrary, your guides know that they must act as friends. And just as you might with any other friend, you're entitled to tell them, "Sorry, I'm too busy to talk with you at the moment," or "No, I refuse to do that." *You* are in control. The guide has no singular power over you and can force you to do nothing.

Guides have a vested interest in being friendly. If in any way they cause you to shun their presence, they'll do what they can to make amends, because to the extent that they prove helpful to you, they help themselves. By interacting with you to your benefit, particularly over a period of time, they complete necessary assignments and gain in stature on other planes of existence. They also gain from the alliance insofar as they're able to work out earthly karma of their own without having to incarnate. One of the guides of a friend of mine was an ex-priest who was endeavoring to inform each of his surviving parishioners that the other side is not as he once preached.

A great deal of the fear associated with contacting a guide no doubt stems from the fact that in our society it's customary for people to invoke the spiritual domain only in moments of pain and urgency. A good friend dies in an auto wreck, a close relative is striken with a mortal ailment, and this is the one time that you feel free to reach across the gate for comfort and guidance. But like a well-constructed ranch gate, the gate between the human world and the spirit world swings both ways, and regular communication can take place back and forth through the opening.

Sometimes communication with a guide is upsetting because the truth is hard to hear. Then again, you may misinterpret a message. Guides do their best to be considerate as well as forthright, but it can be difficult for them to transmit clearly from their world to ours. It's less difficult if they have recently passed on, or if they've been working with you for a while. Nonetheless, if you've ever been married or shared an apartment, you know how easy it can be to get the wrong idea about what another person says or does.

One night I woke out of a blissful sleep. Something had roused me and I glanced around the room. Suddenly, just above my face, two green eyes blinked down at me. At first I was scared; then I got angry. I said, "You know the rules. How dare you appear in that form?" The green eyes, attached to nothing else that I could see, blinked all the way across the room and out into the hall, diminishing as they went. The next night I was awakened by a beam of golden light so beautiful and peaceful that for a while I just basked in it. This time the entity had found the right way to approach me.

Should a guide's presence ever feel discomforting or threatening, simply say, "Thanks for coming, but I don't want you here at the moment and I'd like you to go." If such a statement lacks confidence and proves unsatisfactory, you might resort to a more traditional method. Ringing a bell clears the air. So does the burning of a blue-colored candle. If you prefer a ritual, you might stand and say three times, "Spirit, I mean you no harm; be off!" Each time you say it, lift your left leg so that the knee bends a bit, lightly strike the inside of your left knee with the flat of your right hand, then raise your right hand and flick the fingers away from you.

Remember, at all events, that a guide may never take over your body for any purpose whatsoever—unless (1) you desire to act as a trance medium and (2) you have carried out the physical and emotional preparations necessary for inviting a discarnate being to work through you. This book does not teach you to be a trance medium. Before you attempt such work, you need to be trained by a qualified instructor.

As Elizabeth Haich writes in *Initiation* (Seed Center, Palo Alto, California, 1974): "The [untrained] medium receives all kinds of vibrations but cannot digest them or assimilate them; so he becomes chaotic, unreliable, and weak-willed himself. We should never play with these things! The literature of the field contains masses of sad stories of different mediums who finally degenerated into weak-willed automatons, receiving any and all kinds of impressions, possessing no resistance of their own...."

Types of Guide

Guides are individual beings, so it's rather arbitrary to assign them to categories. Most guides, however, are classifiable according to the depth and duration of your relationship with them. Some share attributes pertaining to their assumed form.

Your guide may be an entity who has never been born into physical form[3] and has never interacted with you before, or it may be someone who has accompanied you in the flesh over a course of several previous lifetimes. It may be a friend of your Source Self, or a friend of your Oversoul (see Chapter 7). Although guides frequently try to gain your trust by taking the shape of somebody whom you'll treasure, your guide may appear instead as an animal or as a mythological creature.

Like attracts like. To the degree that you're finely tuned and spiritually advanced, such will be the guides who come your way. You get the guides that you deserve—based not so much on what you perceive as your current level of spiritual advancement, but on what you have actually demonstrated in past lives, between lives, and in this life thus far. Once in a while you even get a guide who's meant to take you down a notch or two, in order that the experience will provoke you to grow some more.

Lifetime Guides (Guardian Angels)

None of us comes here alone; it is not permitted. We're sent off by senior advisers and arrive in good company.[4] The Holy Spirit has a multitude of emissaries whom we often refer to as "guardian angels." Many times, a so-called guardian angel is in fact a lifetime guide.

While you're a young child, your life guide is a godparent and ally who looks after you almost constantly. The association typically continues on a sporadic basis through puberty and into adulthood, then picks up in intensity during later years. But a life guide won't always stay with you, especially if you demonstrate a preference for working with other guides or if you significantly change your life's direction and emphasis. Life guides may also step into the background if you are presently working with a human spiritual master.

Guides are of particular importance to the well-being of children. In many instances your child's imaginary friends are actually his guides, so don't deny their existence or try to send them away. One of the

---

[3]Guides who have never taken physical form, or whose physical experience has been other than terrestrial, may provide you with abundant information relative to the spirit realm. They may also be a lot of fun. But they're apt to know very little about the limits of human life.

[4]There are numerous references in *Life Before Life*, by Helen Wambach (Bantam Books, 1979), to the experience of being counseled, prepared, and nudged into birth by one or more guides.

worst things that children go through is being told to give up what they know, especially concerning their connections with the world of spirit. Your child needs his guides as surely as he needs you, and as surely as you need guides of your own.

A friend of mine, a psychic in Oregon, told me the following story. She was trying to help a man in his early thirties, a man named Paul who had been emotionally unstable most of his life, with recurrent fits of terrible loneliness. Paul suffered from failure to bond. He was unable to form lasting friendships or develop an intimate relationship with a woman. In the course of treating him, my friend suggested that Paul contact his life guide, and she began working with him toward this end. During their first several attempts, however, neither of them could discern the presence of any guide at all.

One day Paul was describing how, as the only child of an older couple, his loneliness had been compounded. His parents had overwhelmed him with protectiveness ("You're all we've got") and he rarely saw other kids. Then he recalled that long ago he used to have an invisible playmate named Alex. The summer he was four, his family stayed by a lake in upstate New York and his friendship with Alex deepened. They played openly from morning till night.

Then one afternoon near the end of vacation, Paul's parents summoned him into the house. They told him that they'd be going back home soon, and that while Alex had been acceptable as a summertime guest, he'd have to stay behind at the lake when they drove away. Alex could not go with them to the city because he wasn't real, and henceforth they wanted Paul to live only in the real world. Heavy-hearted, the boy trudged obediently outside to find Alex. He relayed the bad news: They had to say goodbye.

As this memory emerged, Paul showed increasing distress. At length my friend said to him, "Why not try calling Alex? Go ahead and see what happens."

"Oh, I couldn't do that," said Paul. "That's over and done with. You can't turn back the clock."

"You never know," my friend said. "Might as well make an attempt, at least."

So Paul called out to Alex as best he could, and then burst into tears of joy as the presence of his guardian angel made itself felt to them both. It was a dramatic case of separation and reunion, the resolution of which soon widened the channel of Paul's life. Eight or ten weeks further along, he had already begun to enter into friendships and form other associations on the human plane.

Other Personal Guides

Some of the guides who help you with your personal life are life-long companions. Others come to you for a more specific purpose, usually to assist with a certain facet of your self-awareness or sensitivity.

Stefan was a single-purpose guide who began by visiting me in my dreams. He represented himself as a little boy, sometimes as young as three, sometimes as old as nine or ten. His message was always the same: he absolutely did *not* want me to be around the man with whom I was then living. Eventually this man and I parted company. But Stefan continued to appear periodically for a year or so after the breakup, still insisting that he wanted me to stay away from my former friend. Since he seemed to be a trickster as well as a pest, I finally called a halt to his appearances and asked him to leave my dreams. He acquiesced.

Another year passed. One evening I went to the movies with my new sweetheart. The film began, and as we sat there in the theater I became peripherally conscious of a rather tall person wearing a plaid jacket and standing in the row to my right. But when I turned to look straight at him, he vanished. This happened three or four times. At last the being took a seat and started to watch the movie like anyone else. His presence wasn't particularly disturbing to me, so I concentrated on my human friend instead.

Two days later, however, I was on my way home from work, and just as I got into my car and switched on the ignition the handsome young man in the plaid jacket forced his way upon me by "coming through the windshield." His face was that of the little boy I'd dreamt about, but matured of course. He said that his name was Steve, and that he wanted to teach me something very important. But I said, "No, thanks," and again told him to go away. I distrusted his all-American looks and, besides, I was still angry with him for persisting in my dreams as long as he had.

Nevertheless, he hung around for the next ten days, desperate to teach me something—or so he insisted. Finally one morning I said, "Okay, teach me what you have to teach me, and then go." At that point he led me to a book by Catherine Ponder, *The Dynamic Laws of Healing,* a book that he'd previously nagged me to pick up. He stood over my shoulder, making sure that I understood certain ramifications of the power of forgiveness: notably, for my work, that forgiveness is the essential ingredient in healing. This was extremely valuable for me to learn, so I thanked him very much and wished him well. After that, I could feel his presence every now and then, but he didn't intrude.

Eighteen months later, I did a past-life regression with psychic Joy Gardner there to coach me. In the lifetime we explored, I'd been married off to a man I couldn't stand, and I recognized our son as Stefan. Stefan was miserable over the way his parents interacted. He sided with me against his father, an incarnation of the same man he had endeavored to separate me from in this life. Following the session, I recontacted Stefan and invited him back as one of my guides. We worked together intensely for about half a year, but now we seldom interact.

Guides for the Day

A guide may visit you for only a moment, to give you a quick infusion of advice. In such cases, to put you at your ease, the guide often appears in the form of somebody you already know or someone you've known before.

My friend Molly was trying to broaden her tolerance for different lifestyles. She had been raised a Mennonite herself, and had turned out a strong, highly principled woman. But she had also grown up with a lot of narrow-mindedness and joyless disapproval. Although she was attempting to be more flexible with her own teenage sons, it was proving very difficult for her to ignore the rules of her upbringing now that her boys were bringing beer home, smoking marijuana on occasion, and inviting girls over to the house.

Molly didn't discuss her inner conflict directly. For quite some time the only clues were her nervous laughter and her frequent references to how strict her mother had been. Her mother had passed on several years prior to this.

One night just before bedtime Molly looked across the room and saw her mother standing there—with a cigarette in her hand. A shock went right through Molly's heart. "Oh," she whispered to herself, "that *couldn't* be Mother." But thereupon she heard her mother say, "Well, Molly, I've learned a few things since I died." With that, the figure disappeared.

In the months that followed, Molly saw no more of her mother. Evidently the one visit was enough. Molly felt certain that her mother had come in spirit to give her permission to loosen up a bit, and this was all she needed to begin viewing her own life and that of her boys with a kinder, less stringent perspective.

Guides for Single Attributes

A guide may be enlisted to help you with a particular attribute that you need to develop. If there is a gap in your life, or if one of the below-listed qualities is not in your repertoire, you can call upon a guide to aid you with just this single characteristic.

abundance	effectiveness	kindness	self-worth
acceptance	equality	knowledge	sensitivity
adaptability	excitement		sharing
awareness		learning	spirit
	freedom	liberation	strength
balance	friendship	love	
beauty			thankfulness
belief	generosity	moderation	trust
bonding	grace		truth
	gusto	openness	
change		originality	usefulness
cherishing	health		
clarity	honor	patience	vitality
compassion		peace	
competence	imagination	pleasure	wisdom
confidence	independence	power	wit
constructivity	inner peace		
		rapture	
dependability	joy	reconciliation	
determination		responsibility	
direction		romance	

Guides for Traumatic Moments

In moments of trial or crisis, a guide may appear in order to help with the particular situation. The guide may assist one person or several people.

Laurence, a college classmate of mine, had grown up in French-speaking Canada as the over-indulged youngest daughter of a widower. Her background was neither practical nor religious. Eventually she dropped out of college and left Quebec for New York, but on the way she was injured in a severe auto wreck near Boston. The retinas of both her eyes were damaged and she required immediate surgery.

During the two weeks following her surgery Laurence was unable to blink, and she was restrained so that she wouldn't move the slightest bit. She knew no one in town and had no visitors. Although the nurses were exceptionally kind to her, her father had gone to Europe on business, so she felt abandoned. She knew nothing of prayer or inner resources. After only a few days, she dropped into a well of lonely self-pity.

About the time she hit bottom, she felt a presence and heard a voice that said, "I am your comforter." And the voice began to tell her the funniest jokes she'd ever listened to, jokes that were completely new to her. This went on for the next ten days, almost a torment of entertainment since she wasn't to blink or shake with her laughter. Not until after she'd recovered did Laurence discover that *comforter* is a term applied to the Holy Ghost.

Some years ago, following a nine-hour drive from California to Oregon, my friend Tina Rosa stepped out of my car and climbed directly into her man's truck. He told her they were taking a sudden trip to New Mexico. John Muir, author and publisher of the well-known manual for VW repair, was dying of cancer at age fifty-nine, and more than three dozen people whom he had provided with timely love and nourishment were now en route to be with him.

Just before the truck pulled out, Tina asked me if our absent-healing group would do what we could to save John. So when the group next met, we tuned in on him and requested special assistance. Two guides appeared who were perceived by most of the group. We recognized both of them: Mattuce, a guide of transport and astral travel, and Esther, a kind, knowing, maternal spirit. They both agreed to visit John and promised to be back in four days. Yet there's freedom in everything. Esther returned, but Mattuce merely sent the report that he was having a wonderful time showing John how to hover over the bed on a level with his friends, how to move around in spirit form, and even how to ride "horseback" through the astral sky. Mattuce implied that the freedom of spiritual movement was loosening John up to let go and die, but this was an implication we did not wish to hear.

Meanwhile, over the following month, I received intermittent phone calls from Tina. Physically, John was getting worse. His death seemed imminent. Shortly after one of Tina's calls I started to meditate, and in meditation I saw a pink star sapphire. I didn't know what this meant, but that evening our healing group met, so I brought the subject up. A young member of the group got the distinct impression that the sapphire was something else that would help John to let go. Once again, however, the rest of us were misled by our hopes for John's survival, and we jumped to the conclusion that the stone might hasten his recovery. Such was the interpretation that I telephoned back to Tina.

Tina and a number of others took the information seriously enough to start scouting around that part of New Mexico. At last somebody found just the right star sapphire and brought it back to John. He wore it for the day in a little bag around his neck; then he died. They buried it with him.

Mattuce kept John company for a month. Finally he returned just in time to be turned over to a thirteen-year-old boy. The boy was urgently seeking contact with a recently deceased grandfather, and Mattuce taught him not only how to stay in touch with a particular relative but also how to work with guides in general.

Mythological Guides

Although the appearance of a mythological figure is rare, it does happen from time to time. Usually the goddess or god is a temporary spirit helper for somebody in need of developing the gifts or special skills for which the deity is known.

A woman might be contacted by a representative of Demeter or Rhiannon, either in human form or in the form of a mare, the animal totem of the earth mother. In most cases, the benefit of having the earth goddess as a guide is that one gains specific information on how to control earth forces and the cycles of nature.

A man seeking mastery of his communicative ability might receive Agni or Hermes, inasmuch as their energy gives one power over the element of fire, which fuels one's capacity with words. The female counterpart of these two gods is Bridget. If you're a man who needs to become aware of his female inner partner, Bridget may be your companion in spirit.

Although these gods and goddesses no longer figure actively in our religious rituals, we all have deep intuitive knowledge of them. Myriad lifetimes have left their legacy in our etheric bodies. A woman who has no conscious awareness of Kwan Yuen, the Chinese river goddess, might dream of her when looking to improve her mothering capabilities or when working to reparent herself. Tara, the Tibetan eliminator of suffering, remover of ignorance, and deliverer of compassion, has been known to sing her chant to Westerners in need of emotional relief but inexperienced in Eastern thought.

As a general rule, a mythological guide is not a life guide. Guides appear in mythical form to help you gain particular skills that you require in order to advance on your path. Whether it be Odin working with you toward courage or Aphrodite aiding you with a difficult sexual problem, your regular guide or guides will continue to help you in other ways.

About one person in fifteen receives guidance from pixies, fairies, brownies or elves. These small devas are not of the human order. If we let them, however, they can help us grow plants, heal children and other living creatures, make handcrafted objects, arrange physical comforts, and attract financial well-being. Many years ago in England —where they're not thought to exist—I was surprised to see leprechauns, who specialize in teaching practical applications of creative powers and unusual talents.

People who meet up with small folk commonly interpret the event as a kind of divine reassurance. The meeting place for the elfin world and our world is an undisturbed natural environment. If your desire is to form an association with one of these folk, go to the forest or the desert or an isolated meadow, and after meditating, follow the invoking procedure outlined earlier in the chapter.

Totem Animals

Although animal spirits are quite different from the guides experienced by most people in our culture, they are well-documented in American Indian lore, legend, and practice. According to some tribes, each person has two totem animals. You may replace a particular totem animal with another after having incorporated the qualities of the first one into your character. Other tribes believe that a person's totem animal is a gift from the Great Spirit. Once you receive it, it is yours for life.

Some Indian groups have a tribal totem—often a main food source. As part of their spiritual practice they pray to this animal, dress to resemble it, and emulate its strengths. California Indians used to hold bear dances. Tribes in Alaska do a snake dance every few years to help them let go of those who have died, so that the discarnate souls may be peacefully ushered into the spirit world.

A totem animal serves principally as a guide into and through the dimensions of the unknown. In *Never Cry Wolf*, an elderly shaman describes to Farley Mowat his first momentous excursion, while in the company of wolves, into the world of dream and trance. Mowat has himself been living amidst a wolf family, partaking of their life to the point of eating what they eat: mostly mice. As he listens to the shaman's tale, he acknowledges his own between-worlds experiences with his family of wolves. Traditionally, the wolf is a pathfinder—the creature who leads human beings through the doors of everyday perception into other realms, and toward a cosmological understanding hidden from most people.

In *The Way of the Shaman* (Bantam Books, 1982), Michael Harner discusses animal guides at some length. "Through his guardian spirit or power animal, the shaman connects with the power of the animal world, the mammals, birds, fish, and other beings. The shaman has to have a particular guardian in order to do his work, and his guardian helps him in certain special ways. The guardian spirit is sometimes referred to by native North Americans as the *power animal*, as among the Coast Salish and the Okanagon of Washington. This is a particularly apt term, for it emphasizes the power-giving aspect of the guardian spirit as well as the frequency with which it is perceived as an animal. But the Coast Salish also sometimes refer to the guardian spirit as the *Indian*, for it can appear to them in human form as well."

Experiences with totem animals lie deep in the racial memories that we all share. These memories are most vivid in the newly born and in the dying, both of whom are tenuously connected with the earth plane. Lost hikers, people on psychotropic drugs, the very ill, and seekers of higher consciousness are also good candidates for finding themselves in contact with an animal who talks, shows them which way to go, or permits them to merge temporarily with the animal's form. People have reported that, while in spontaneously attained trance states, they have flown in the body of a bird, or swum deep underwater as a fish, or bounded along the ground in the form of a jackrabbit.

Young children often encounter their totem animals in dreams, dreams which are sometimes frightening. The animal may appear extra-large; it may try to come closer and closer. When a child awakes from a dream like this, the well-meaning parent tends to rush in and provide assurance of ordinary reality. What the child needs, however, is the reassurance that it's natural, when small, to be scared of communicating with the agents that foster one's higher self. Children commonly have such visions between the ages of four and seven, a period of time when their guides are reaffirming the life work they are to do and the path that they're to take.

In many cases the memory of these visions is lifelong. A young woman who has attended several of my classes distinctly remembers a series of dreams that occurred before she turned six. In her dreams, she was carried on the back of a turtle. For quite a few cultures, the turtle represents the earth. The Hopi call our planetary home Turtle Island.

Bears, snakes, hawks, whales, deer, wildcats, dolphins, otters, and other undomesticated animals also serve as totems. The deer is seen as a healer and as a brother on the path. It represents all our relations (mother, grandfather, friend) rolled into one. A person whose totem is the deer is destined to spend this lifetime interrelating profoundly with other people, often acting as the central figure or counselor in a family, a circle of friends or a community.

Very seldom do domesticated horses, cattle, chickens, or geese act as one's totem animal. Sometimes, however, a guide appears as a stray dog that draws your sympathy and ends up becoming your pet. Befriending a dog or cat can trigger a personal renaissance and open your heart chakra.

Birds frequently deliver messages that are straight and to the point. Ba, a bird guide from Egypt, taught me to construct a "psychic pyramid"—a procedure for focusing energy so as to help bring about events on the material plane. In assisting wishes to come true, this procedure has turned out to work on deeper and more potent levels than the affirmation technique.

The eagle is said to be the only animal that can look directly into the sun. A person who has earned the privilege of having this intensely different life-form as a totem has powers of clairvoyance, clairaudience and clairsentience far beyond the ordinary. As a consequence, one can take a more direct spiritual path and know God as few sentient beings do.

Family Guides

In a class that I gave during the spring of 1980, there was a young matron named Renata, born and raised in Italy. Renata was devoted to the doctrines of her religion and upbringing, but she was also haunted by a powerful psychic talent. She had four guides, all of whom were apparent to me and my assistant; yet she was unable to open up to them, no doubt fearful that if she did so, she'd blow up her entire belief system. Of the four, the guide who impressed me the most was Bartolomeo, an Italian musician of the thirteenth century. I described him to Renata, but she said that she'd never encountered him before. Nor did she even recognize the description.

Upon returning home after the class, Renata shared her experience with her sister Lucia, including the rather exasperating information that evidently there were several guides just waiting for her to get through to them. In particular she mentioned Bartolomeo, the musician. That very night Lucia had a vivid dream in which Bartolomeo spoke to her in Italian. He told her that for hundreds of years he had served as a guide to her whole family, and especially to the women. He'd helped her great-grandmother and her grandmother, and now he was doing what he could to help her and Renata and their female children. He belonged equally to all of them.

Although by age seven I was aware of the presence of numerous discarnate beings in my vicinity, my own first spirit contact on a conscious level was with two family guides, one from my mother's side and one from my father's. My mother never talked about her guides, either the personal or the family variety, until I was grown up, but whenever they were around I could feel their energy and smell their aroma. Despite her reticence my mother did work with her guides, however, and she also interacted with some of the guides that accompanied my father, though he himself chose to ignore them. At the age of twelve I acquired the habit of coming home after school and sitting in my late grandmother's suite of rooms until one of my father's guides delivered a message.

Family guides watch over family destiny. They monitor the life path of each individual and that of the family as a group. They rescue unwary children, especially under-fives and teenagers who wander into the track of disaster. They also take stock of the accumulated karma that family members have come together to work out. In this connection, they do what they can to weed out disruptive in-laws and to arrange marriages with persons who will make a stimulating or harmonizing contribution to family affairs, above all as regards the accomplishment of projects that the guides hold dear.

5
FIRST ENCOUNTERS
AND ENDURING ALLIANCES

Report by Lynn K. Steffen on a spirit-guide workshop given in Eugene, Oregon, April 25, 1981.

As I lay there searching for my guide, someone touched my right cheek and I sensed a presence at my right side. Shortly after this, though I still lay flat on my back, I felt that a being much larger than myself was hugging me around the shoulders from behind, encompassing and filling me with a great depth of peace and love.

Then a name came to me: Mary Anne—a name I don't happen to care for. I saw a tall, gaunt woman with dark hair pulled severely back. Her dress was as long and plain as she herself, with sleeves to the wrist, a white bibbed apron and a floor-length skirt. She wore no adornment. I understood that she was a Shaker.

In my mind I asked her, "Why are you here?"

"To teach you to trust again," she said.

This set my thoughts awhir. Early in life, I had learned for various reasons to withhold confidence from others.

I asked whether she was planning to help me in some further way.

"You must learn to love yourself," she replied. "There are people whom you love; but in order to love them more wisely and in order to trust yourself with them more completely, you'll have to start giving a lot more love to yourself."

"For my own selfish benefit?"

"For everyone's benefit. Learning to love yourself is equivalent to achieving freedom from your troubles and hangups. Without their distraction you can get on with your life's work and serve the world more effectively."

"What's my life's work?"

"You know that already. To teach and heal, heal and teach."

Next I inquired if we might have known one another before. There came two replies: first, that we had been playmates and lovers in a long-ago time and place; second, that more recently, in late nineteenth-century Europe or the United States, we had been twin brothers.

Later on, when I went for a walk with my guide, I saw a cat in a window and as usual thought "Ugh." Mary Anne commented that she has always been fond of cats.

Across the street I noticed a church-like building. Actually what attracted my eye were the shrubs that surrounded it, a profusion of azaleas and rhododendrons in bloom. But after admiring the flowers for a while, I realized that I was on the front lawn of a convent. Mary Anne then informed me that she had spent a life in a convent, in addition to her celibate life as a Shaker. I began at that point to reflect on the difficulties of celibacy. In response to my thoughts, Mary Anne went on to say that, in her case, the celibate lives were to make up for the excesses of intervening existences. I asked her to be more specific, and she indicated that she'd tell me about this at some future date, but not just now.

Notes by Mary Anne Gawf, following a spirit-guide workshop given in Eugene, Oregon on July 18, 1981.

Jeremy Burg; Irishman; fourteenth or fifteenth century.

Strong and stalwart, lusty and sweet. Roamed the moors and knew the leprechauns.

Neither peasant nor prince. A squire who preferred freedom to a life of settled leisure. Had material wealth but was indifferent to it and finally left it behind.

A charming rascal: mischievous, a high sense of humor. Hair either black or red; eyes green or blue. Smartly dressed but not chic. Favored russet-brown and green. (The day of the workshop I wore a shirt of russet, gold, green, and black.)

Loved and understood animals, Knew many secrets of the earth. Had a great longing for the wide-open, windswept moors, a longing which I share. In part, my decision to live in Oregon, the Emerald

State, stems from his enthusiasm for the climate of the Emerald Isle. "Soon now," says Jeremy, "people shall delight in differences and in kindred spirits."

His purpose is to teach the art of appreciating *everything* in life, including the riches that he scorned. Most important: cherishing the beloved, to keep me from dying of a broken heart like Aunt B----. This I know to be true.

He'll help me to acquire the material abundance that he abandoned out of indifference. My poverty cycle is broken; meeting Jeremy put a hole in it. I don't want to be rich except in what I desire and choose to value. Mainly I want to learn to appreciate creatures, both human and animal, and what they give to me—even when their gifts are objects.

Written statement by Kevin Kiper, radio operator, Cocoa Beach, Florida.

I suppose the first time I acknowledged a spiritual guidance or guide was when I was about ten. I began to notice that, when I mulled over a decision, there was a little voice or verbal chatter within me that said,"Don't do it," or "Yes, that's right." Sometimes the voice had a soft, reassuring tone. At other times it was a stern, abrupt command.

The spirit was a female presence whom I later learned to call Azibeth. As I grew older I realized that Azibeth would not always suggest what seemed to be a logical alternative. Therefore I would often ignore her advice—though afterwards I would usually wish that I hadn't.

One time Azibeth saved my life. In the fall of 1978 I made a plane reservation with the intention of seeing my father in Chicago. I was to fly first from Sacramento to San Diego, to have breakfast with my aunt. From there I'd take another plane to O'Hare International, where Dad would meet me.

As I boarded the plane in Sacramento, already full of excitement about seeing Dad, I was surrounded by other passengers bustling here and there, settling themselves and their possessions into their assigned places. A flight attendant spoke to me about my seat, but I didn't really hear her. I was listening instead to what Azibeth was suddenly starting to tell me. She said, "Get off this plane right now." So I did.

On September 25, 1978, that same 727 collided with a Cessna over Lindbergh Airfield and all the people in both planes were killed. Furthermore, the crash set fire to several houses, thereby raising the fatality count. It was later said to have been one of the worst air accidents ever. I may have missed breakfast with my aunt, but I also escaped a certain death.

After this incident I fully realized that Azibeth does exist. She watches over and protects me. When she talks to me, I listen. Although I'm an active person and like to take part in sports that some people consider dangerous, I've never been seriously hurt. Whether or not anyone else credits my fortune to a guardian spirit, I'm glad for the protection.

The lessons I've learned from disobeying my guide's advice are also important and valuable to me. If I've learned the lesson, I'm able to heed her warnings as they come: "You know better, you've been through this before" (meaning in this life or maybe in a former life). For example, in my present life I don't really have very many material desires, and I've found that it suits me to be non-aggressive as an approach to getting what I want. It appears that, at least in part, I learned the validity of both these qualities from a previous existence in which I was overbearing and acquisitive.

Every now and then I temporarily forget about Azibeth. When I do, it seems that I lose touch with my inner peace. A lot of her work consists in showing me to myself. She tests me sometimes, but exposes me only to conditions and situations for which I'm ready. When I can handle a situation responsibly, she opens me to a little more. Even as I sit and wonder which way to go, she gives me patience to make the right choice and take the right step at the right time.

From a tape-recorded statement made in July 1981 by Janice Stewart Volkmer, psychic reader and adviser, in Santa Cruz, California.

My guide seems to be a Franciscan friar. As I've perceived him over the years, he wears a brown robe, a rope belt, and sandals on his ailing feet. He's emotional but very gentle—a Cancer-type person, astrologically. (My rising sign is Cancer.)

I experience him to the right of me, at "two o'clock," a couple of feet away. (Two o'clock is also my favorite time of day.) He speaks only into my right ear. My left is my telephone ear. Clients have brought it to my attention that when I do a reading, I incline my head to the right. I try not to, but it just happens. In fact I'm doing it at the moment.

The only instruction I've ever received in psychic work has come through my guide. Though he communicates no more than a few words at a time, the messages he gives me are loud, sometimes very loud. I first heard him speak to me back in 1970 or 1971. I was baking cookies, waiting to take them out of the oven, when suddenly he said to me, "For of the ways of others ye shall know." I couldn't believe what I'd heard. I said, "What?" And he repeated the message.

Soon after that my doctor came over to pay me a medical visit, and on his way out he remarked, "You know, Jan, I think you have a certain gift, and I wish that you'd try to do a reading for my wife and myself." I said I'd be delighted. And that kind of started the wheels rolling in connection with my present work. I had done sporadic readings prior to this, but the scope of my efforts had been as limited as my confidence.

I'd never before been approached by a spirit entity, not even during my childhood. I used to daydream, I liked to exercise my imagination, but more for the sake of making plans or looking ahead to actual occurrences. I never kept company with an invisible fantasy-being who advised me on what to do next.

After my guide contacted me, however, my psyche started to grow and my whole life gained in depth and significance. That was the real beginning of my "ministry"—or whatever it is that you enter into when you provide psychic counseling and try to do the best you can. When my mother died in 1980, I was so heartbroken that I thought I'd quit reading forever. But I couldn't stop. I'd walk down the hallway of the house and my guide would envelop me in words of support and encouragement, just enough to keep me going.

He's always been a comfort to me. Whenever I get to feeling bad, it soothes me to see and feel his presence or to hear him speak. He told me in advance of my mother's passing over, naming a date and a day of the week that I checked out on the calendar. The foreknowledge was unsettling, but when it proved to be true my faith got a little boost that helped me in my grief.

For the most part I get personal messages when I'm totally alone and my mind is at rest. Yet I believe that my guide is in contact with me continually. It seems to be up to me to throw out a question every so often and then wait expectantly for the answer during one of my alone times. We all need to work at being clearer, more open receivers for the loving presences that volunteer their services. And we have to verbalize our desire, or it's just not going to come.

During readings, my guide alternately stimulates and reinforces me so that I'll keep wanting and striving to do better, not only for myself but for others. To this end he surprises me with many kinds of information, including pertinent names and numbers. At the start of a reading, for example, he may give me the birthdate of the client who has just sat down in front of me. Relaying this sort of information is fun for both the client and myself. It creates a memorable first impression and forms interest in psychic work.

Working with guides takes us into the whys and wherefores of the transmission of thought. It may be that our current guides are entities-in-spirit of who we used to be. The fact that we're able to blend so harmoniously and thoroughly with the energy field of another being suggests that they might be previous incarnations of ourselves. Then again, in keeping with the idea that we are reborn into roughly the same circle of family and friends, they might be passed-over relatives, from this or a former life. At any rate there seems in some way to be an important connection between your present guide and your past lives. I get the impression that my guide appears in the guise and garb of a friar because, until seventy years ago, my family were Catholics living in Austria.

I used to feel that I had just the one helper. Now, however, I may be getting my recently departed mother as a second guide. I've been hoping that this would happen. This past month she approached me in a dream (or perhaps it was an early-morning vision), radiant and beautiful. It was a joy to feel her presence once again.

When we tell God what we want, He's much more likely to bring it to us. So I'm not discounting the possibility that we can call up our guides. But I think the calling up has to work two ways. I don't believe we can just summon an entity to come—not unless he or she already intends to do so and has a true message.

I call my guide St. Bernardore. Now and then I see something like a chalice of braided silver in his hands, something that holds a cup but isn't itself the drinking vessel. The strips of silver braid are woven diagonally to form diamond patterns, and there's a short stem. To me this is a symbol of his vast spiritual resources. Over the past year I've had to withdraw from people to some extent, in order to regain inner peace and strength. In recovering, I thank the Lord that I've been able to rely on the love and energy emanating from this being by my side.

Written statement by Joy Gardner of Victoria, British Columbia, author of *Healing Your Family* **(Bantam Books, 1982) and** *Healing Yourself* **(Healing Yourself Press, 1977).**

I met my first guide during a Spiritual Journey (a form of guided meditation) with Helen Ram in Seattle, Washington. I saw a winding road that connected the earth and the heavens, and along this road came a Chinese man, dressed in flowing robes magnificently embroidered with mountains and trees and other scenes from nature, which he also seemed to embody. He spoke to me through his garments, his gestures and his presence. His name was Chow Minh.

Thereafter, Chow Minh reappeared to me at various times when I needed comfort or strength or reassurance. But he rarely communicated in words.

In 1977 Laeh and I were returning together by car from a healing gathering where we had been teaching. Since her workshop had been about spirit guides, I stared recounting my experiences with Chow Minh. I lamented that he hardly ever spoke to me verbally. "Well," said Laeh in her typical offhand way, "throw him out and get another one." So disrespectful! Of course I wouldn't throw out my beloved Chow Minh, but it hadn't occurred to me that I could have more than one guide.

Evidently this new idea took root rather quickly, because after I dropped Laeh off at her house and continued the hour-long drive to my place, I began to experience another presence in my car. The being who now introduced herself to me was a modern woman of the last century. She was extremely talkative. Her only common ground with Chow Minh was that she too liked to wear long, flowing attire. She was an elegant, powerful lady. I felt in awe of her.

Her name was Mae, and she had been a madam. She ran a good house and was respected in her town. She said that in her day there wasn't much else a powerful woman could do. I enjoyed my new guide thoroughly. She was always there with helpful advice when I needed it, particularly in matters of love.

My third guide came into my life when I went with a friend to a meeting of the Spiritualist Church. Not knowing what to expect, I was rather surprised to find myself at a seance, with one man acting as medium. In the course of the meeting, he channeled in several guides (including Madame Blavatsky) who are well-known to Theosophists. Each of these guides spoke directly to some of the people in the room.

At length the medium channeled in Dr. Lang. I believe that Dr. Lang was a surgeon in the late 1800s. In any case he directed himself to me. He saw that I was very skeptical of what was going on, and he asked me to be more open-minded. Then he asked if there was anything he could do for me.

I had been traveling by car from eastern Washington to Seattle. My back was tired, and I still had to make the drive up to British Columbia. I mentioned this and Dr. Lang said he'd take care of it. I tried to be open-minded, and found that by the time the meeting was over, my back felt much improved. Then, as I drove north, my back got better instead of worse. I was quite amazed.

Perhaps it was my amazement that opened me to the possibility of Dr. Lang's existence, because he soon started talking to me. When I say that a guide "talks" or "communicates verbally," I don't mean that I hear a voice outside myself. It's more like hearing thoughts that are not my own, or like dreaming about being spoken to by someone.

I liked Dr. Lang immediately. It was easy to trust him, and I'm still learning from him. He frequently visits me when I'm driving alone on long trips, and will talk for as long as an hour at a time. In fact, he has taught me a great deal about color healing—information which has proved very effective and which I have not encountered in any of the books on the subject.

6
WORKING WITH YOUR GUIDE

Everything you know about interacting with other people applies to working with guides. It's a relationship, and it reflects all the many facets of your human relationships—marriage, friendship, family arrangement, business association.

Don't forget to be kind to your guide. Say thank you for all assistance. At the same time, recognize that working with a guide is a two-way street. Guides can do favors for you, but you return the favor. They're drawn to you and cooperate with you because you're capable of doing what *they* want to have happen in this world. There are guides for astronauts and elevator operators, for socialist reformers and lifetime Republicans, for atheists and traditional religionists.

We tend to treat guides as if they were so much more perfect than incarnate beings, as if they were all-knowing deities rather than helpful friends in spirit form. We act this way because we want to believe that it's true, just as we once wanted to believe that our parents had limitless insight and ability.

Even master guides don't have a handle on the whole universe. The validity of their information varies with the area of expertise. Franco is a master guide of healing, but once when I tried to consult him on a matter of geography he went blank on me. He didn't know any more than I did. However, since his guidance is impeccable, he admitted to the gap in his knowledge and set off to research an answer to my question.

Some guides—usually life guides—are particularly attentive to your wants and needs. They notice that you're hunting for a bit of information, and either they volunteer it to you directly or they arrange for you to bump into some manifestation of it as you pursue your daily routine. You must keep in mind, even so, that while guides can broaden your informational base and support your intentions, it's still you who has to make the choices and decisions regarding the course of your life. Your guides cannot and will not live your life for you. Nor do they have all the right answers ready-made.

Keetoowah, a Cherokee medicine man, likes to quip: "Dead don't make you smart." And the "dead" are perfectly aware of this. If you find and start working with an earthly guru, your guide may feel superfluous and back off. However, if you've become entangled with a false mentor or with somebody who's not right for you, the guide's activity is almost sure to intensify.

Message for a Friend

A good exercise to begin with when working with your guide—an exercise that can increase your contactual and cooperative skills at a rapid rate—is to request a message for a friend. Ask in a concentrated way, but don't specify which friend you want the message for. Your guide will either picture the recipient or state a name. You'll also get a bit of very clear information, perhaps relevant to a subject about which you had no prior knowledge.

Then go to your friend and tactfully convey what you've been given. If your friend is open to phenomena such as guided advice, relate the whole truth. If not, you can always say something like: "You know, I was thinking about you yesterday, and it suddenly occurred to me that..."

Some time ago I had to resort to indirect tactics in dealing with an infertile couple. Tom, the husband, had previously been through a hurry-up marriage to legitimize a baby son. When the marriage broke up, he was left with the child. Although Tom had never professed doubt that the boy was his, there was that lingering suspicion. Then he married again. His second wife turned out to be a good companion to him as well as a loving mother to her five-year-old stepson. She was unable to conceive, however.

During a session with my guides, one of them recommended that Tom have a sperm count. I asked why. Because, said the guide, this course of action would serve as a releasing mechanism. On a prove-it level, it would erase his underlying doubts about his capacity to be a biological father. So the following week I suggested this. When the sperm count showed normal, his wife confessed that one of her secret fears was that a child born to them would look so different from her stepson that Tom would think he wasn't the father. Indeed, as it happened, the son she subsequently bore had reddish-blond hair, unlike either parent or the members of their families. (Some of our worst fears are self-created illusions; others are accurate or distorted premonitions of things to come.) But since Tom had already been assured as to his ability to father a child, he could safely ascribe the discrepancy to a genetic quirk.

Maureen, a woman who has done spirit-guide work with me, received a message for a friend of hers who was perpetuating two notably negative patterns: she was terribly overweight and she continually wore black. According to the guide, the difficulties of the overweight friend stemmed from her dread of her own psychic power and her efforts to conceal it from others. Maureen called me up, wondering what she should do. I said, "Tell her you just got this crazy idea that, for some reason, a psychic training class might help." It did.

A related exercise is to ask your guide for a clue to the world situation. In workshops, it's not uncommon for people to get messages about large-scale events which make little or no sense at the time. Yet within the year, much of the information proves correct. Christopher, who attended a class in December 1977, reported via his guide that the weather would be unusually harsh that coming winter. In January 1978 there were extensive frosts in Florida and it snowed all the way to the Bahamas. Ruth, a class participant in October 1978, talked of a surprising breakthrough in the Middle East crisis. There followed the treaty between Egypt and Israel drawn up at Camp David in April 1979.

For further practice with this kind of request, check the list of "borrowable" guides in Chapter 10. Note which guide has the expertise to help you with a current problem and call upon her/him by name. State the precise nature of the problem and, if possible, the kind of solution you would like to arrive at. Chances are that you'll receive advice inwardly or that you'll find yourself led to an outward circumstance that triggers the answer.

Asking for Favors

When you have a particular need that you can't seem to meet on your own, whether it has to do with a job or a personal commitment or a question about the workings of the universe, try bringing this to your guide's attention. The answer to your question will depend partly on your guide's store of knowledge and partly on your receptivity. If you ask about the afterlife and your guide happens to know little about the many levels of discarnate existence, you won't get a very clear or detailed reply. The reply will be further muddled if you have deep-seated fears in regard to death and dying, or if you're resistant to experiencing life in all its dimensions.

However profound your guide's information may be, it's your responsibility both to follow up on the advice and to use your own judgment. Suppose you have a legal problem and ask your guide to direct you to a competent attorney. Even when your guide has a background in law, it does no good to hire the suggested individual unless he turns out to be somebody with whom you feel a rapport. Of course, once you and your guide have come to know and trust one another, it's unlikely that you'll be directed to someone inappropriate. But it can happen. So if the lawyer who's been recommended doesn't suit you personally, tell this to your guide and discuss the basis of selection. Although the guide may evade your probing, you don't have to settle for short, pat answers.

Suppose instead that you have already retained an attorney, yet feel unsure about your choice. Your guide, whether well-versed in the law or not, has the advantage of being able to check with a deceased lawyer of note concerning the validity of your selection. You might also have success with regrounding and attempting to contact the former lawyer yourself, or possibly with contacting a close lawyer friend of your own who has passed on. Neither approach will work, however, if it comes too soon after the entity's transition. You may have had a strong personal connection with the lawyer friend, and he may well be looking to contact you too. If he's a very close friend, or an intimate family member, continuing contact is often a matter of course. But, in general, interaction with a human being is disturbing to someone who is newly deceased. First of all, he's busy processing the material of his recent physical life and readjusting to life as a spirit. Second, your appeal re-animates his attachment to earth, and you do him a disservice to pull him back—rather like placing an urgent telephone call to somebody who has finally mustered the courage to move away from home to another state.

When you ask your guide for a favor, be patient if you don't get an answer right away. Your guide hears you whether you declare your desire aloud or keep it to yourself. If you're badly in need of a certain object or want very much to locate someone who's been hard to track down, your sharp-witted companions will read your thoughts; and more often than not, in the weeks and months that ensue, they'll somehow arrange an encounter between you and whatever or whomever you seek.

Letting Your Guides Put Things in Your Path

A number of years ago I got pregnant unintentionally. When I understood that I was pregnant, I became very upset because I was no longer living with the father. I wanted to have the baby, yet the father and I weren't getting along at all.

So there I was, physically stressed from being pregnant and emotionally wrought up, as if all the electrical circuits in my body had been cross-wired. It was a likely time for something critical to happen.

I decided to take a trip with some other people to the California Sierra. On the eve of our departure, my mentor Essie Parrish came to me in a dream. In addition to being a Pomo Shaman, Mrs. Parrish was an expert basket maker; and in the dream I was at a big outdoor sale looking over some Indian baskets. Essie Parrish appeared and handed me a basket. On my way home, however, the basket got damaged somehow, and then I lost it. This bothered me deeply. I wanted to go back to her and get another one, and yet I knew that she couldn't afford to be so generous again, since her baskets were expensive. Nor could I afford to buy one.

I found the dream very disturbing, both while it was going on and after I woke up. I knew that, among the Pomo, it's against the rules for a woman to make a basket while she's pregnant. So I was aware that the dream symbolized the breaking of my "basket" of pregnancy. But I chose to ignore the message.

A few days later, during our stay in the Sierra, my friends and I drove to a Quaker gathering in Nevada City. All the way to the meeting I ate Hunza apricots and the kernels of their thin-shelled seeds. By the time we reached Nevada City, I was staining and my body felt just terrible. About a week and a half later I miscarried. It wasn't until several years after this, while sharing office space with a midwife and an obstetrician, that I learned that apricot seeds are an abortifacient.

When I got back home, my former man-friend wanted to have it out with me. I avoided him and kept the miscarriage a secret. But I was still angry with him, and unable to deal with the anger. Then I had another dream. In the dream, my man-friend kept pigs, and I wound up killing his prize sow. I awoke in a turmoil, thinking, "No, not the sow. It was *him* I wanted to kill."

That morning it was sunny and the day warmed up early. I went out into the meadow beside the house. Suddenly I spotted a yellow book, face down. This surprised me because my young daughters and I lived by ourselves on 36 acres, and I didn't have visitors who lay around in the meadow and read books. Despite the hour the book wasn't soaked through. In fact, it was barely wet with dew. I picked it up. It was Frazer's *Golden Bough*, open to the section on the sow-goddess, worshipped for her fertility. And now it came clear to me: I was angry at the man's capacity to father children so easily. It was his fertility that I wanted to damage, not him.

The Golden Bough was full of other information for me—so much so that it seemed to be a gift dropped out of the sky. My guides know I'm a book addict, and no doubt that's why they have consistently arranged for me to discover the right book at the right time.

Guided Planting

If you have a guide who is knowledgeable and enthusiastic about green growing things, take him/her with you when you go gardening. Spirit helpers can show you exactly where each flower and herb, each bush and seedling vegetable should be planted in order to thrive. They know which soil conditions need improving, and they'll often give you wonderful suggestions as to plants that you might include.

Along this same line, guides can assist you to choose plants at a nursery. They see the luminescent glow around the healthier specimens, and they'll teach you to notice it too, through their eyes.

A guide with a green thumb will let you know when it's time to plant and transplant. Don't feel silly if you're out there digging in the dirt at 4 A.M. The metabolism of some plants is least threatened if they are unearthed and re-earthed at that hour. Guides can supply many kinds of information pertinent to the science of planting and transplanting—indicating, for example, how much sun comfrey needs or which phase of the moon is correct for disturbing lettuce at minimum cost to its vitality.

Rama Burns, a friend of mine who's a yoga teacher, told me the following story. "Across the road from the house we've been living in for the past seven years, there's a small patch of miner's lettuce. Miner's lettuce is our children's favorite wild edible herb, and in previous springtimes I have patiently waited to include this special gift from God in our salads. I always wished there was more of it, however. Last year I finally communicated this wish aloud as I gathered the plants. This spring miner's lettuce is popping up everywhere. The flowers of miner's lettuce are usually white, but these are lavender—to me a sign of their spiritual origin."

Guided Tours

Whether you normally enjoy the outdoors or not, plan an excursion on foot, a walk in the country. Or, if you're a city dweller, take a stroll through a rose garden, along a riverfront, or across a bridge. As you proceed, let your guides stop you where they will. They give you pause so that you'll get a deeper and clearer look. The view is often two-way: Something lights up for you externally and, in the same moment, your inner being opens and you glimpse your own light within.

A walk with a guide can be pure bliss, an avenue to some of your best learning. Perceive an array of tiny flowers and you may feel the wholeness and oneness of all creation, feel your place in the universe whose life force courses through you. In this fashion, you rediscover the exuberant intimacy with earth-life that you experienced when you were a child and everything radiated some sort of magic.

The awareness that you are at one with the universe, and the peace that accompanies this awareness, is a form of meditation. At some point in your walk, your guide may also nudge you into a more familiar meditative posture: lying in the grass or on a park bench, sitting back against a tree or a railing.

Another adventure is to take a guided expedition through a strange neighborhood. Turn left or right according to your inner voice. If you're told to climb to the top of a jungle gym, don't worry about looking ridiculous at age forty-two. Just follow the suggestion and see what happens.

A woman friend of mine was led to sit beneath a foot bridge in a city park. She started listening to people as they plodded, strode, and skipped over the bridge. After several minutes of this she began to deduce the age and health of each pedestrian from the quality of the footstep. On a more profound level, she furthered her appreciation of how a part reflects the whole.

Another acquaintance, a lady named Catherine, decided to take her guide to the supermarket—an exercise that I recommend in class. Catherine said it was one of the funniest shopping trips she'd ever been on. She would reach for an item and the guide would say, "Put that back; you can get it cheaper elsewhere, I'm sure of it." If Catherine put it back, everything was OK, but if she left it in the cart they'd argue up and down.

The guide pointed out two women who were shoplifting. The comment was "You really want to eat for less?" In the checkout line he kept her laughing with trenchant observations about the salespeople and the other shoppers. Then, since enough was enough, he helped her settle down by reminding her to do the self-healing technique that he'd already suggested for empty intervals such as this.

Guided Playing

Many adults in our modernized culture—and, indeed, many adolescents—are remarkably uninventive with their time when off the job. We learn to lose ourselves in pastimes such as card-playing, drinking, gossiping, watching television, shopping, and pursuing various other paths to momentary gratification. Often we feud with friends and relatives, not because there's anything to fight about, but just to alleviate the boredom.

Overeating, smoking to excess, taking drugs and hanging out, and pouring energy into any of the well-known war games are all ways of avoiding a life that is creative, pleasurable and self-aware. We encounter suffering everywhere; we suffer ourselves. Yet our fear of letting things be different—our distrust of being able to live in a free-flowing, fulfilling manner—keeps us trapped in the very situations that we agonize over.

Perhaps what we fear most, in connection with savoring life, is that we'll do something crazy and then be ostracized. We come equipped with a heritage of stern, anti-emotional policing. Having fun is frowned upon and often forbidden by religious or civil law. Our culture is still debilitated by the tendency to emphasize the negative a great deal more than the positive.

In a psychic development class one day, everybody began to crack up, unable to restrain their hilarity. As the laughter continued to reverberate around the room, a woman about fifty gasped, "Oh my God, we'll laugh so hard that next thing we'll start to cry!"—a statement that led to a discussion of the cultural taboo on releasing a full spectrum of emotions. The taboo exists because such a release is one of the most profound ways to exercise power. More important than this, however, it is an expression of intense vitality that undoes long-held emotional damage and brings on freshness of spirit.

All too often we pass up opportunities to let our work be play—or to let it be a growth experience that yields deep joy and contentment. A schoolteacher can have an exciting, satisfying career; or she can get bogged down in conforming to a work schedule and to the state-approved lesson plan, so that her interaction with children has as little spark and liveliness as the routine of someone who solders electronic components day after day.

The job doesn't matter—be it research chemist, homemaker, graphic designer. When it becomes dull, rarely do we confront the problem directly, since this entails revamping our attitude or searching for another job. For the most part we tend to harden up or to retreat, to forget quality and go for the big bucks or to daydream and feel resentful. Some of us create compensatory excitement by living in a perpetual state of crisis or paranoia. Others circumvent the issue by sleeping eleven hours every night.

At some point nearly all of us find ourselves in a dead-end pattern —staying up till 3 A.M. doing crossword puzzles, eating cookies and reading old magazines, packing the hours with styrofoam activities. The next time this happens to you, approach your guide for help in getting you out of the doldrums. Most guides have a wealth of knowledge about play, either from their human experience or from the playing they've done on the inner planes.

My friend Jack has a life guide named Jerry. For about fifteen years Jack had been marginally aware of Jerry's presence, but they'd never met face-to-face or conversed verbally until Jack attended a spirit-guide workshop I was conducting. Jerry manifested as a grey-haired but zestful man in his mid-forties. He sat in a wheelchair due to an accident that had befallen him in his youth, an accident that was essentially the result of self-neglect and a grim outlook.

By nature eager for warmth and approval, Jack grew up learning that the rigors of life are supposed to exceed its pleasures. Jerry became concerned that, as an adult, Jack might well be another candidate for a wheelchair or the equivalent. As a consequence, his main purpose as a life guide has been to encourage Jack to play, especially in ways that involve his physical body. Behind Jack's present involvement in soccer, roller skating, and dance-band music is Jerry, wearing off Jack's sharp edges and urging him on toward more outlandish forms of physical activity the older he gets. In the process, Jack has learned to appreciate and care for his bodily self. In general he's become a more relaxed and playful person—mentally, emotionally, even sexually. His basic earthiness, no longer so pent up, now has a joy factor that makes it more acceptable.

Jerry is one of those guides who make their presence known gently. By dipping here and there into Jack's cognitive mind, he helps on a subliminal level to call forth situations that will permit Jack to go on growing. Jerry's human life was fairly recent, so his contributions blend easily with Jack's earth-plane consciousness. Carefully, subtly, he instigates dreams, visions and flashes of information—understanding that, were he to be in some way obtrusive, his charge would only react with stubborn opposition. As it is, although Jack has begun to open up to Jerry on occasion, he's still reluctant to admit that his creative work and his lifestyle might be other-directed to any significant degree.

As is the case with many people, my own main guides don't happen to be at all playful. Sometimes you need to ask the universe for an additional guide to help you specifically with play.

Andrew is a serious-minded physician who provides emergency-room care. He's devoted to his patients, basically full of compassion for hurt and death, and able to deal with the seamiest, most desperate sides of life. But after several years his enthusiasm began to wane, dampened by repeated exposure to the bare-survival atmosphere that permeates most emergency rooms.

Andrew found himself drawn to spending days off by the seashore, which was a considerable drive from his residence. He would sit on the beach for hours, or walk up and down. Nights he spent safely in his cab-over camper.

One day while trudging aimlessly along the shore, he spotted what appeared to be a moose beneath some trees up on the bluff. The moose saw him look and moved off into the brush, just out of view. Andrew clambered up the bluff and began to follow, heading inland. These days, it's unheard-of to encounter a moose in western Oregon. Andrew tracked it avidly through the woods and heavy underbrush of the coastal hills. Though the moose kept at an elusive distance, never did it attempt to escape entirely from view.

Nightfall found Andrew in unfamiliar surroundings, far from any of the roads he knew. He located a patch of dry ground and covered himself with leaves and pine needles. In his down parka he was warm enough to manage a fitful sleep.

He continued to follow the moose for two more days. He watched what the moose browsed on, and ate what he thought he could assimilate. On the morning of the fourth day, just when he thought that he finally had the moose in plain viewing range, it disappeared over a rise. He gave chase and came out on a paved road. There was no trace of the animal.

Disappointed and disheveled, yet elated by his adventure, Andrew abandoned his search at that point and hailed a passing car which took him back to the beach. It was only as he started to drive home in his camper that he realized he'd missed his shift at the emergency room. He was more delighted than chagrined.

When he arrived, a box awaited him on his front doorstep: a gift-wrapped present from his sweetheart. Andrew opened the box. Inside was an exquisite carving of a moose.

Although Andrew visited the beach frequently thereafter, he caught sight of no animal larger than a deer. But in the meantime he had begun to acquire a passion for spending time outdoors and living off the land. He is now an experienced backpacker and woodsman.

It occurred to Andrew, even as his adventure was unfolding, that the shadowy moose might not be a flesh-and-blood creature but a guide sent to infuse a measure of gladness into his life. As it turned out, he didn't need a change of work. Caring for the sick and injured is his true path. But he did need to refresh his sensitivity and rediscover the pleasure of existence.

Asking for Dreams

When you feel trapped by an ongoing situation and desirous of advice or clarification, ask your guide to bring you a relevant dream. In many cases the dream will come to you the first night. If it doesn't, repeat your request at bedtime for the next two evenings. At that point, should you still be unsuccessful, let the matter go. Rest assured that a dream will reach you later on when the time is right and you're in a better position, mentally and/or circumstantially, to accept its message.

Carol Alena Aronoff is a highly developed psychic with a doctorate in psychology who practices in the San Francisco Bay Area. She specializes in various forms of dream therapy and guided imagery. During the early 1970s she helped to found the SAGE Project, a program of holistic and humanistic therapies open principally to senior citizens.

For almost three years Carol and I lived in the same county and saw quite a bit of each other. One season the county went through a late-spring buildup of pollen and air particles that was particularly harsh on asthmatics and people with allergies. Carol suffers from recurrent asthma and was among those affected. Once asthma sets in, it's generally very difficult to treat in oneself, even pharmaceutically, so Carol asked me to assist her with the healing process. This I did on several occasions, but each time the symptoms would return.

In the interim we talked at length about interacting with guides and about the feasibility of seeking spirit counsel with respect to alleviating and curing physical ailments. Carol finally decided that since she had been working so long and so intensively with dream incubation, it would be easiest and best for her to request guidance by way of a dream.

Here, from her journal, is the dream that she received shortly thereafter:

"Laeh is getting married at the Blue Heron Inn. I go to the wedding and end up talking to two waitresses about allergies. One of them suggests that we find out more on the subject and invites me to step into a back room. The room has a window, and outside the window some plants are growing. The waitress points them out. I recognize miner's lettuce and skunk cabbage and name them aloud.

"The waitress reaches out the window and breaks off a piece of skunk cabbage, offering it to me and recommending that I eat it. I demur, protesting that the plant isn't good to eat and may even be inedible. Nonetheless she advises that I ingest it for the desensitization of my allergy."

Carol telephoned me early the next morning, full of elation and curiosity. Laughing, she told me about her dream. Though we were both experienced herbalists neither of us had ever heard of anyone using skunk cabbage to treat asthma. A few days later, however, Carol was leafing through an herb book to find an herbal preventative for her son. The book flopped open to the page on skunk cabbage, and she discovered to her surprise that the roots and seeds were listed as an antidote for asthmatic spasms, with the cautionary proviso that one guard against the toxic effects of an overdose. Since the plant wasn't native to our area, Carol bought some from an herb distributor. It helped to keep her free of symptoms for the rest of the season.

The following spring, the asthma returned. In an effort to get to the core of her trouble, Carol meditated and asked her guides for an image of what was going on in her chest. She envisioned a ballerina being spun in circles by a male dancer—around and around. It was this image that Carol began to work with. First she had the ballerina move away from the male dancer and spin by herself. Then she had her gradually slow down, come to a stop, and take a strong, grounded, independent stance. The reshaping of the image proved to be the key to the relief of Carol's asthmatic problem.

A guided dream can also help someone else who's in trouble. A woman named Phyllis was sent to me by a mutual friend. Alan, her three-year-old son, had been badly hurt in an accident, his spine fractured in several places. The physicians in attendance weren't at first sure that they could repair his injuries or that he'd ever walk again. The boy remained cheerful, however, despite being in the hospital and immobilized by a body cast.

We visited Alan, and I was struck by the physical resemblance between mother and son. Both had dark hair, sensitive green eyes, and flashing white teeth. They were personally very close and often communicated nonverbally.

Throughout our visit Phyllis shared in the boy's cheerfulness. It wasn't until we arrived at my house that she let on how stressed and tense she felt. During dinner our conversation was further complicated by the fact that she wasn't the kind of person who confides easily in others. I wondered how in the world I could help to lighten her burden.

That night while meditating I asked my guides for assistance, but nothing came. Then I fell asleep and had the following dream:

Phyllis is kneeling before an altar or shrine dedicated to her dead child. I stand there watching. Then I kneel beside Phyllis and there appear two guides, Cosmos and McGregor, with whom I was working at the time. They remain, but the atmosphere and sensations of death are washing over me, removing me disturbingly far from life. Phyllis and I are to learn more about death. We're in a column of some sort; inside, it's completely dark. My body expands and expands until it's too much for my ego to take. My ego-consciousness halts the process and draws me back to wakefulness.

After I go back to sleep, the dream resumes, but this time without the aura of death. Phyllis and I are in a room of my new house. We observe a black finch that has been trapped indoors; it dashes itself against a window, trying to get out, exhausting itself.

A man comes in and speaks to us; meanwhile the finch flutters behind a curtain. When it flies out again, it has been transformed. Now its color is a mottled mix of grey and beige, and its head plumage is unique. The man catches it and holds it. Then he and I talk. We agree that he'll leave the bird, but will come back to pick it up the next weekend.

I related these two dreams to Phyllis when we met again. She sat and looked at me with a stunned expression.

"Did anyone tell you that I had another young child who died?" she asked at length.

"No," I said.

"I never grieved for him or even looked at his body. My husband took care of all the funeral arrangements."

I suggested that she call psychically upon her dead child and that she articulate the yearning she had repressed for so long. A message of this sort, I assured her, would readily travel between the two planes of existence. It would be heard and appreciated.

The second dream seemed to be a prognosis for Alan's recovery. By all indications, the man in the dream was an idealization of Phyllis' husband. In contrast with his willingness to assume responsibility for the ordeal of burying their first child, he had been too busy with his career to help much with Alan. Phyllis had been the parent on call, and she'd been forced to negotiate singlehandedly with the doctors and the hospital.

Yet if it was up to her, there was no escaping this. So with my encouragement she set up an appointment with the head neurosurgeon. To her abundant relief, she learned that Alan's fractures were beginning to mend, that his spinal column was intact, and that he had proper sensation along the major nerve routes. His return to full health would only be a matter of time.

Mindful of the dream, Phyllis asked the surgeon if Alan might be able to go home the following weekend. The surgeon said yes, weekend visits were all right, as long as everyone in the family understood that Alan would have to be cared for closely for some time to come.

The Take-Away Person

Nurses in many different hospitals have noticed that, at the time of death, a patient who has been weak or even comatose may suddenly start to speak quite loudly and lucidly with someone not visibly present. Those whose loved ones pass away at home often observe the same phenomenon, a phenomenon that can also affect a family member who is senile or semi-conscious due to accident or illness. In most of these cases, the family member is heard talking—or mentions having talked—with someone, now deceased, to whom they were once close: perhaps their mother, or a sibling, or a childhood friend. In 1842, Ralph W. Emerson's son Waldo died of scarlet fever at age five. In 1882, when it was the father's turn to make the transition, his friend Bronson Alcott heard him call out, "Oh, the beautiful boy!" just as he had done at little Waldo's deathbed forty years before.

The conversations that the dying have with their take-away person are deeply significant. The take-away person is a discarnate being whom the dying one trusts,[1] a being able to provide reassurance during the crossover period when personal and acculturated fears can combine to hamper natural acceptance of the transitional process, a being who can pick up the nuances of the dying person's emotional condition, mental state, and level of energy. The two enter into an intimate

---

[1]Sometimes the take-away person is actually a master guide who has gained permission to act as a surrogate for the trusted being. A master guide is very likely to be the take-away person for someone with whom there has been cooperation over a period of years.

confidence. Information is funneled into the person about to be trans-formed (how to move through walls, for example, and how to travel astrally)—various kinds of preparation for life without a body. For those whose death is swift the take-away person acts as an anchor amid the confusion of the initial adjustment period.

The experiences reported all over the world by people brought back from clinical death indicate only the opening of the doorway. Following the welcome home, what goes on in the "corridor" and in the "waiting room" (as several newly passed-over guides have termed these stages in the transformational process) is rather like a debriefing session. Instruction continues, but the main emphasis is now on re-exploration and detailed examination of the lifetime just past. Master guides (see Chapter 11) reveal forgotten knowledge and coach the new arrival in self-analysis. When the debriefing has been completed, the guide helps the soul to begin a satisfactory level of work, frequently a resumption of the work they were doing before seeking human form.

The more aware you are of the spiritual world as you live your physical life, the easier transition will be for you. Jesus the Christ serves as the take-away person for many who know and love Him. When Gandhi was shot, the word which fell from his lips as he slipped away was "Ram," the Sikh term for the one God above all.

Cosmic Cops

Several years ago I put out a request for a guide to help me with some research for a proposed book. I needed a guide who was in an advanced *loka*,[2] one who was beyond having to reincarnate.

That night as I lay in bed, I looked out the window into the trees and saw the face of a man. He seemed to be signaling to me that he was the being I sought. I asked his name. He gave it as "Calvin," along with the dates of his last lifetime (his birth happened to occur exactly a hundred years before mine and took place a hundred miles away). I switched on the bedside lamp to enter all this data into my journal. The signs seemed auspicious and I was excited, yet I also felt an under-current of unaccountable misgiving.

When I turned the light back off, Calvin had vanished. So I called him once again. As he reappeared, more clearly this time, I suddenly realized that this being was in fact the tormentor of two unhappy peo-ple with whom I had been marginally acquainted for several years.

---

[2] *Loka*, a Sanskrit word, refers to quality and degree of being. It also conveys the col-loquial sense of the word *place*.

Vern and Roberta were chronic victims of ill luck regarding their place of residence. One spring as they slept through a heavy rain, the rising waters flooded their basement and garage, causing structural damage that forced them to move. Thanks to the Red Cross, they found a trailer to rent on sixty acres of land. Only two weeks before my encounter with Calvin, however, a November windstorm had sent a tree toppling across their trailer, destroying it along with many personal possessions. They then took a cabin adjacent to friends of mine. Within days, their stove blew up, and that very evening the toaster caught fire, enough to scorch the cabinets above.

My first response to Calvin's actual identity was to fill my little house with light and to ask my two main guides to come to my side and give me extra protection. Then I asked for information. What was the story on this being who had so kindly introduced himself as my research assistant?

I learned that he was a husband of Roberta's from a previous life. Their marriage had been childless, and Calvin was obsessed with envy at her present fecundity. As a consequence, he'd set about to sabotage her happiness in every way he could.

If Roberta and Vern had been inviting less difficulty into their own lives, Calvin's influence would have been limited to something like cracking a bedroom window with a hailstone. But despite their good points, they had serious problems. In general they thought that the world owed them everything. In combination with their basic lack of self-confidence, this attitude led to their habit of floundering around, soliciting advice as to what they ought to do next. The result was that Calvin was able to afflict them with inimical events.

Although my contact with Calvin lasted no more than ten minutes, I was infuriated that he had tried to fool me in order to gain my trust. So I sent for the cosmic cops; I asked that they appear. Mentally, I blew a whistle and pictured a very strong, moral being coming to my aid. The cop turned out to look like one of the Smith brothers on the coughdrop box. I saw him take Calvin by the shoulders and haul him away.

Cosmic cops truly exist. They're entities who have power and know how to use it. They're not at all pushy or cruel, but they're adept at taking care of any spook who tries to make trouble in the physical realm. If you sincerely need them, they'll come, manifesting as anything from an English bobby to a Japanese samurai, whatever costume inspires comfort. And they do their job well. Five months after my confrontation with Calvin, Vern and Roberta were both working gainfully. They still had their problems, but their housing situation seemed to have stabilized.

Guided Predictions

Most of us have very little faith in our capacity to visualize the future or to dream prophetically. We don't trust our ability and often we're afraid of the process. It tends to frighten us when we have a dream whose details are crystal-clear or that turns out to be at least partly true in waking fact.

A member of my own family is convinced that he'll die if he's made aware of the life work remaining for him to do. It's not uncommon for people to be scared that, if all their karmic debts are paid, they'll be called back to the other world and forced to drop their body.

Some people are disturbed by the *I Ching*, by Tarot cards, and even by meditation, because these techniques give them access to information on the vibrational planes, where patterns of reality are first revealed. Given our cultural orthodoxy, we're so accustomed to screening out this kind of information that we fail to let ourselves in for a lot of advance knowledge that could be useful to us. Tarot, astrology, and other divinatory procedures are under the protection of archangels who keep the unready from access to more than they can handle.

With regard to prophetic activities, a guide can serve as your shield and filtering device, as well as a temporary proxy for some of your own power. Consider the following example.

One morning after meditation, my life guide Johannah came to me briefly and announced, "You're going to learn a new skill." I started rummaging around in my head, trying to figure out what skill she might be referring to.

The next evening a member of the Redwood Forest Meeting, a Friends' group, called to enlist my aid in locating the child of an acquaintance. I explained to her that this was not my forte—that psychics have particular talents, and mine did not include finding of lost objects or missing persons. I did feel that the boy was alive, and I mentioned the state where he might be living, but rather than presume to go any further with it I redirected her to a specialist in psychic search.

A few days later I was visited at the office by a client in her seventies, sent to me by her physician to see if I could assist in bringing down her high blood pressure. In conversation, I learned that the woman had recently mislaid a collection of jewelry that she was going to pass on to her daughter-in-law. This seemed to be the cause of her turmoil. As usual in these cases, I called on Johannah for help.

"You're on your own," Johannah said, floating away almost as soon as she appeared. "Time to develop that new skill."

I looked within and saw a dresser drawer where underwear was kept. The drawer itself was partitioned by a couple of dividers. I described this to my client but it didn't register.

Since my mother, Doris Garfield, has a flair for locating lost articles, I consulted her on the phone. "I'm no psychic, Laeh," she said to me. "All I do is picture what I might have done with the object if I were the person in question."

"Could you please try that now?" I asked her.

"Won't do any good," said my mother knowingly. "She's too wrought up over it. That lady's never going to find her jewelry until she gets her blood pressure back down."

So I began to do a daily series of absent healings with my client. A week and a half thereafter, she telephoned to say that she had just sat down to do some sewing when unaccountably she stood up again and walked through the house to a tall dresser that she rarely used. "Sure enough," she said, "the top drawer of the dresser was divided into three sections. And some time ago I did store underclothes in it. Anyway, I reached inside, and guess what was there?"

The new skill that Johannah forecast didn't emerge all at once, though I continued to receive requests from people in need of this line of service. I even got involved in an attempt to track down the victim of a homicide, but I shied away from the demands of formal detective work. After two years, however, I'm much better at pinpointing the whereabouts of lost possessions, especially papers and documents.

Guided predictions may relate to your career or to minor events in your life. Keep a record of all of them. Note down the date of each prediction, the identity of the guide, and the content of the advice.

A guide's information should be correct about 85 percent of the time. If a prediction proves inaccurate, or if following a suggested course of action doesn't pan out smoothly and advantageously for you, bring in your guide and discuss the discrepancy. Sometimes the guide turns out to be the ill-informed source. At other times the inaccuracy is the result of your own misinterpretation (see Chapter 12). If, after a careful reading of Chapter 12, you still find yourself unable to receive a guide's messages clearly and correctly, you may have to seek the assistance of another spirit, one who understands the limits of your communicative skills and can help you more effectively with prophesying and planning.

7
CO-BEINGS, SOURCE SELF, AND OVERSOUL

Beings and Co-Beings

Contrary to the scientific belief stystem, and to some religious belief systems, the personality does not die along with the physical body. Following an interval for rest, review of life events, and self-examination, the personality continues to exist and be active.

The discarnate being is somewhat diminished in comparison with its corporeal manifestation. It is much less egotistical for one thing, particularly as regards matters of earthly consequence. Certain information falls away because it's no longer pertinent—just as the adult "you" loses conscious touch with the intensity and actuality of the emotions you had as a child. Other characteristics remain fairly intact, however, whether the personality has been discarnate for one year or five centuries. Eventually, of course, it mellows as it becomes exposed to the manifold experiences of subsequent co-beings.

Each of us is a distinct human being. Yet each of us also belongs to a family of co-beings whose individual personalities and life dramas interconnect to form a larger experiential whole. Co-beings enjoy a shared memory and a shared sense of self.

In recent years humanity has started to broaden its tolerance for unorthodox ideas of how the universe originated and how life works. In the process, many of us have grown more receptive to the possibility of reincarnation. Some have even begun to explore the memory bank that they share with their co-beings. Those who undergo "past-life regression" generally find that the procedure clarifies their present existence and helps them get to the roots of personal behavior that has perplexed them until now.

One myth concerning life after life is that male/female definition fades and the personality becomes asexual. It may be true that, in the world beyond, physical events such as playing tennis, eating apricots, and having sexual intercourse do not take place. But the discarnate being continues to manifest a gender and to retain an intellectual perspective based in part upon that gender.

The tendency of a discarnate personality is to get softer and gentler, although an extremely strong being may have trouble relinquishing its grosser features. Other personalities have to be encouraged to maintain their integrity, either because they're weak or because they suffer from the misconception that one drops everything at the moment of death.

Over time, a personality's force may subside, but it retains all its chief talents and shortcomings. As we have already seen, the strengths and failings of a spirit guide can spill over into your current life. If you're a house builder and your guide was a medieval artisan who devoted his life to working on a cathedral, you might have a penchant for Gothic windows and arched doorways.

This same kind of influence, relating both to technical style and to focus of enthusiasm, flows between one co-being and another.[1] If one of your co-beings was a first-rate mathematician, you may have a flair for mathematics even though your own gift is weaving and dyeing, an occupation in which patterns and quantitative figuring are important but heavy theorizing is not. On the other hand, successive lifetimes often turn out to be quite diverse. The chaste soprano in the church choir could have been preceded by a co-being who was a streetwalker on New York's Eighth Avenue. The grim but loyal family provider might be followed by a co-being who is irresponsible and hedonistic, yet wonderful to his children.

The lives of co-beings fit together somewhat like the segments of an orange. Unfortunately, the common image of reincarnation suggests lives strung together like beads on a string. This linear distortion leads to the mistaken conclusion that there is a hierarchical ladder of

---

[1]Spirit guides also get input from *their* co-beings, but this information is not of the same profundity as that of their own incarnating experience.

incarnations or a rank-structure of life roles, and that a lifetime as a priest or a spiritual healer cannot possibly follow a lifetime as a drunken roustabout or a bloodthirsty mercenary. The social result of this error is a caste system of one sort or another.

To understand the entirety of our many lifetimes, we have to transcend moralistic doctrines that deny the divinity of every stage of being. All lives are stages on the path of growth. The life of the prostitute can provoke as much learning as that of the greatest physician. We are all divine sparks, irrespective of our earthly station.

Source Self and Oversoul

How is it that you can be connected to so many others and still be yourself? That you can manifest the talents and traits of previous incarnations yet remain a distinct person? That we are all one, yet individuals?

There is a universal system of beings, a nondenominational, nonpolitical, family-like affinity group originating with God. All beings participate in this arrangement — as colleagues, as elders, and as youngsters. The being who keeps closest watch over us is our Source Self, roughly analogous to our mama. Actually, the Source Self is the integral as well as the generator of oneself and one's co-beings.

A mother can have many children, each of whom demonstrates physical, emotional, mental and behavioral characteristics that reflect her maternal influence. If a human mother consistently speaks in firm but gentle tones, rarely raising her voice, that same quality is apt to be evident in all her children. In like manner, the notable traits of a Source Self are transmitted to all the co-beings who incarnate therefrom.

The Oversoul is the Source Self's source self. Each Oversoul also has an oversoul. Your Oversoul is comparable to your grandmother, your Oversoul's oversoul similar to a great-grandparent.

Like your biological mother, your Source Self herds you about, trying to point you in the right directions and suffering over the pain you might be putting yourself through when your life could be so much easier. Your Oversoul, in grandmotherly fashion, prods your Source Self to do a bit better and provides both of you with sound, practical wisdom born of long personal experience and the many lifetimes of her numerous progeny.

A Source Self also has the deeper maternal quality suggested by expressions such as "mother tongue" and "mother earth." The quality of mothering and the family atmosphere that results are comparable to the effects of speaking a particular language. A particular mother tongue has its range of tribal experience built into it, its areas of expressiveness and expertise, and its areas of vagueness and ignorance. It's hard to grow beyond the parameters of a native language without learning the use of a second tongue. Such are the limiting aspects of your Source Self, your Oversoul, and even your personal spirit helpers.

There is also an expansive aspect to your tribal connections with the other world. If your co-beings, Source Self, and Oversoul are all Demeter-like (earth-oriented, and with the look or feel of earthiness), your special strength probably resides in your groundedness and your abundant appreciation for nature. If your Source Self resembles Athena, you can usually rely on wisdom and practical incentive, regardless of your circumstances of birth.

Meeting your Source Self feels much like contacting any other guide. Getting in touch with your Oversoul, however, is a unique event. Have you ever felt pure love—no judgments, no conditions or restraints—just love for love's sake? An Oversoul is considerably removed from earthly life, having reached what is often called nirvana and therefore having no need to incarnate again. Yet your Oversoul is brimming with love for you. Although you must be thoroughly grounded when you meet your Oversoul, thoroughly open and fearless, it is a joyous as well as a solemn occasion: like a loving family reunion, but infinitely deeper and sweeter.

The best method for attempting to communicate with your Oversoul is first to ground and meditate, then to strengthen your aura, and finally to create a psychic pyramid of luminescent, translucent gold. A psychic pyramid is a tool for raising yourself to etheric levels.

Seat yourself beneath the pyramid, in the very middle. Leave your emotional concerns and mental designs outside, and fill your heart with glad anticipation. If you're mentally or emotionally turbulent, contacts you try to make on the etheric level will be greatly impeded. Hostility toward other people can bounce back at you extra hard.

A psychic pyramid glows. Make sure that yours has this radiant quality before proceeding to work within it. When all is as it should be, ask that you be given your Oversoul's name. In most cases the name will seem utterly alien to you, and you may well have difficulty catching it precisely. The sounds may not transcribe easily into written English, so ask to see it spelled out.

Oversouls are not necessarily androgynous. They often maintain a very definite gender, speaking to you in the most resonant and mellow tones of their chosen sex.

My own first awareness of an Oversoul occurred while I was meditating deeply one morning. Into my mental space there came a name, and somehow I knew that it belonged to my Oversoul. Though the sound of the name was barely intelligible to me at the time, I found out later when learning Sanskrit terms that it means "Lady of Inner Knowing." As soon as I came out of meditation, I wrote the name I'd been given in my journal so that I wouldn't forget it.

Several weeks thereafter, a guide who had been working with me for a few months contacted me during a tune-in and said, "It's time you met your Oversoul. We'll do it next week."

The following week I was busy teaching classes and readying a large presentation. I lost track of the day. Eventually, after my usual morning meditation, I realized that more than seven days had elapsed, so I sought out my guide. My guide happened to be in a tremendous hurry. His own most recent incarnation had ended only a few years previously, and now he was preparing for the imminent transition of his former earthly brother. But he hastily directed me to get into the psychic pyramid that I'd been taught to use.

My Oversoul appeared. She floated into view dressed in a gown that shimmered with interchanging pinks, blues and purples. I was surprised to see a female form—surprised and skeptical. I had read and been told that beings of oversoul status were androgynes who could take the shape of either sex, in an effort to appeal to their various offspring. Yet at the same time I was awestruck by her extreme gentleness. She had more strength in that gentleness than I have encountered in anyone before or since—such an unlikely combination of qualities that I could scarcely believe it.

"How come I'm so hard when you're so soft?" I asked her.

With a little wave of her hand, she replied, "It's just a learning place; just a learning place."

I tried to rephrase the question in my mind, thinking in terms of a character defect on my part. But she kept on saying, "It's just a learning place." There was no trace of displeasure or any other negativity. The only emotion that emanated from her was total love and acceptance.

Within myself I vowed that I'd grow to be more like her. She was listening to my thought, and she let me know that her support was in accord with my wish.

I asked her if she would take care of a health problem of twenty years' standing. She passed her hand-energy through my body, commenting, as if I were a clay model, "We made a mistake in the neck." I could feel the adjustment as she made it. It felt like hand energy, although it certainly didn't involve a physical hand.

Now there was no holding her. Suddenly she was gone, and I was unable to call her back for anything further.

Since our first meeting, I have contacted my Oversoul rather infrequently, perhaps because our initial interaction was so significant and complete. Occasionally I reach her presence for a few moments, but only when she's ready and willing and I truly need her intervention.

Working with Your Oversoul

An encounter with your Oversoul may be brief, but the meeting can be the occasion for an exchange of such importance that the duration of earth time is irrelevant. Your Oversoul can heal you, indicate the main purpose of your life,[1] point out a path toward a firmer commitment to your purpose, trigger a burst of enlightenment, and otherwise enrich and broaden your existence in ways you'd hardly dream possible.

On the other hand, your Oversoul will not show up every time you step into a psychic pyramid. An Oversoul ministers to thousands of needs throughout the universe, and will interact with you only when circumstances are appropriate. Don't ask your Oversoul for trivial things like a promotion, or a new car, or recovery from a minor illness, or success with a love object who has currently caught the glint in your eye. Refer such matters to your guides and companions.

The most valid reason for contacting your Oversoul is to get help in identifying areas within your Self that need deep work. If your life is diminished by a deep-seated emotional fix[2]—a fundamental personal problem that you may have been born with—your Oversoul is definitely the being to turn to when all else has failed to remedy the situation. What happens with most of us is that our life-energy follows the path of least resistance. Often we're so trapped by the familiar pattern of our emotional fix that, without the intervention of an Oversoul or a good teacher, or without a profound inner desire to change, we tend not only to act it out from birth to death but even to carry it on from lifetime to lifetime.

The patterns we get stuck with in this life frequently originate with instances of forfeiting power in previous incarnations—for example, death at the hand of another, or failure to draw emotional support from those we trusted. In our current experience we may at-

---

[1] As human parents, we can provide an analogous service to our children by trying to help them remain (or become) conscious of their present life purpose.

[2] The major emotional fixes are: stinginess, fear, worry/doubt, boredom, resentment, cajolery and flattery (self-betrayal), vengefulness, pretense, lust (greed for sex, money, fame, or material things), and victimized loneliness or martyrish passivity.

tempt to relive the moment and emerge victorious. Some of us become soldiers, co-being after co-being. Others are bonded to addictions that are not cast off by physical death. If we die an alcoholic, alcohol is the very thing that we're in danger of succumbing to early in our next lifetime.

Traumatic events in our most recent lifetimes account for the majority of our irrational fears in this life. The focus of our fear may be a tense situation, a piercingly loud noise, a wild animal, or a certain type of personality. In any case, we run into difficulty; and our response to the difficulty is usually one of avoidance. If a co-being of yours was a doughboy who died in a trench somewhere in France, there's some probability that at age ten, when all the other kids were happily jumping in and out of a newly dug drainage ditch, you reacted hysterically.

Avoidance behavior is futile, however. Not only does it fail to eliminate the fear; it actually perpetuates it. Fortunately, fear-patterns of recent origin are fairly easy to undo by means of skillful psychic work or by way of psychotherapeutic methods such as Jungian analysis, dream therapy, neurolinguistic programming or gestalt techniques. The important factor is that the psychic or therapist be right for you.

On the other hand, the patterns that have the most tenacious hold on us are those generated by co-beings furthest away in linear time. Crucial events in these "distant" lives are apt to be so far removed from our current consciousness that, even with the aid of therapy, we cannot perceive them as precursors of whatever form of craziness we've presently taken on. Nonetheless, answers and solutions may come by way of deep meditation, a spiritual master, an advanced psychic—or from your Oversoul.

During one of my morning meditations, a guide approached me and announced that he was a long-ago incarnation of Rocky, a man with whom I'd been acquainted. For as long as I'd known him, Rocky maintained a harem of paramours who resided in neighboring counties. His harem was the light of his life. Certainly his infidelities and absences weren't betrayed by a lack of ardor.

Rocky's pressing need for multiple relationships had always puzzled me. The spirit shed light on the riddle. Appearing in his earthly guise, with a mane of steel-grey hair and a red cap resembling a fez, he told me that he had been blessed with six wives and had loved them all. This pattern had been passed on to Rocky, who was ill-fatedly trying to live it out in the context of twentieth-century Western culture. As a result, he found himself in alternating states of emotional confusion and compulsion in regard to his many women, struggling to keep things going with two or three while stepping out to make the next conquest.

Unaware of what he'd inherited from his ancient co-being, Rocky simply couldn't adjust to a social setup that demanded monogamy. He did know that at some level he needed input and clarification. He even sought out a guru. Yet when given pertinent information, he had a hard time absorbing it. He just wouldn't—or couldn't—change his ways. At one point I suggested a session with his Oversoul, but he didn't seem to think that this was an option.

One of the reasons why people fear death is that, during their current lifetime, they've been shunning or shying away from the personal growth that they were intended to do on the inner planes. In the afterlife, once the initial period of homecoming and joyful greeting has passed, there remains a long uphill pull for those who neglected the deeper game in the earthly world. Meditating and dreaming on this subject often makes me cry because I realize that people who die without attending to their life's work are wasting a precious human existence. In so doing, they bring about a suspension in the unfoldment of their being. Their Source Self may forgo incarnation entirely for a while. It might saddle them with the role of a froufrou housewife who fritters her life away but longs to *do* something, or that of a man who is so indecisive that others end up making all his life choices for him. Or it may churn out a near-duplicate co-being, born into similar circumstances—over and over again, if necessary—until the Source Self and all the co-beings have come to terms with the experience.

8
QUESTIONS AND QUANDARIES

I like the idea of working with a spirit guide, but how do I know that what I'm getting isn't just my runaway imagination?

This is a good question, one which is asked in every class—first, because everybody who might be interested in working with a guide is naturally concerned about being able to distinguish between the true and the false; and second, because everyone knows somebody who suffers from an overactive imagination and reports all sorts of odd data, often including conversations with discarnate beings.

I've worked with clients whose imaginations were harmlessly overactive, who needed mainly to be reassured as to the conscious practicality of the process (rather than experiencing it as a state of mind that they lapse into guiltily and involuntarily) and instructed in correct preparation for use of the imaging skill, which entails the thorough physical grounding and inner clearing described in Chapter 2. I've also worked with clients whose imaginations were running dangerously out of control. One young man heard agents who tapped into his every thought and transcribed these thoughts to TV producers; he'd then watch TV and feel personally exposed by things that happened on the programs. Here again, grounding and clearing were essential to his reorientation.

A true guide gives you information that is verifiable and that proves to be advantageous—information that you would have access to in no other way. Above all, a true guide is your friend and comforter, supporting your efforts toward all the life goals you've been born to seek. The products of a troubled imagination work to one's detriment and that of others. One feels tormented and pursued.

Often the signs of a true guide are sensory details that impress you, that somehow soothe and satisfy you deeply. Do you smell and taste the presence? Does it pull you away from your attention on everyday things? Or is it just a flash? As noted previously, your guide may have a distinctive tone of voice or give off a subtle aroma—sensory particulars which you're unable to duplicate by self-suggestion when the guide is not present.

One more thing. If you get a famous guide, avoid reading their biography or written works, at least for a while. Otherwise you'll confuse the actual messages that you receive with the messages that you give to yourself, and then you'll conclude, quite rightly, that you've been making it all up.

Suppose there has been someone in this life whom you loved and who later passed on. Can this person now be your guide?

Irene, a lady who had recently celebrated her eightieth birthday, disclosed during a class that, some twenty years before, her husband had come to her in spirit not long after his physical death. Throughout a difficult second marriage Irene continued to feel his presence. She never thought to address him directly or to request anything of him. Yet his proximity always brought her peace of mind.

At the time of the class, Irene was in vibrant health, with a sweet nature and a lively sense of humor. She credited much of this to her ongoing relationship with her first husband, adding that in the future she looked forward to calling upon his wise counsel, just as she used to do when they were man and wife.

It's also possible for someone to be alive and serve as your guide. An advanced soul who has recently resumed flesh may well act as an adviser and helper when their small child's body is napping or asleep at night.

Can a former incarnation or co-being of mine act as my spirit guide?

Yes. In the universe, we never die. Nor do we reunite as one big soul. Our very creation as a particular entity gives each of us perpetual freedom. We're free to interact with anyone else, even a co-being— perhaps especially a co-being. It makes sense that a previous incarnation of yours might display great interest in your current life and could exert a profound influence in your behalf.

Are my spirit guides inside or outside of me? My therapist insists they're inside.

This question reminds me of a story told to me about Essie Parrish, the master shaman and master teacher. In 1965, at Esalen Institute, she had a dramatic run-in with Fritz Perls, the father of gestalt therapy, over the same issue. In the course of conducting a seminar, she was describing how spirit helpers work. Perls, then in residence at Esalen, happened to be sitting in on the workshop. He interjected that one's guides, such as they are, exist inside, not outside.

The shaman didn't know Perls, and at first she believed that he was simply misinformed. She patiently explained several times how and why a guide must definitely be an external entity. Her firmness on this point so angered Perls that he flew into a rage. She remained composed and self-possessed and avoided a shouting match. However, one of the full-time participants at the workshop, Carlos Castaneda, did respond. Perls fumed off.

On the last afternoon of the seminar, the director of Esalen brought Perls back to the class in hopes of making amends. Essie Parrish was polite but stood her ground. In an effort to demonstrate that spirit companions are beings in their own right, she used special sounds to call each of her healing helpers and her other guides, one by one. "You see," she said, "each guide responds only to its own sound."

Once again Perls boiled over with rage, shouting out that Mrs. Parrish was not only deluded but completely wrong. Again, Castaneda came to her defense. At the breaking point, Perls slapped Castaneda across the face. Castaneda reacted by wagging his forefinger and saying, "You naughty, naughty boy!"

Psychotherapists are often people who have shut themselves off to the mystical along with rejecting the obvious nonsense of occult charlatans. Some are tolerant of reported spirit contact, but very few have bothered to develop their own sensitivities to the extent that they are able to distinguish between the discarnate voices a sane client is trying to understand and the relentless din of voices that plague a client who is mentally disturbed.

A therapist with a keen, well-trained intellect may make admirable insights concerning human affairs, but this is no reason to accept his pronouncements on the realities of the world of spirit. Even theologians are apt to be far better informed about religious doctrine, moral precedent and church history than the subject of interacting with spirits, one-to-one. Although you may find support for your perceptions from recognized experts, you may have to rely on the details of your own experience to conclude that each guide is indeed an individual self, a distinct and external entity.

Periodically I go to a psychic lady. She contacts my guide for me and passes along advice and suggestions. I'm unable to find or talk to my guide without her. According to her, this is how my guide wants to relate to me.

Self-appointed intermediaries frequently live out the ancient role that pretends to be of service but actually seeks to dominate. The fact is that you're meant to have personal access to, and personal attention from, your spirit friend. An honest psychic will introduce the two of you to each other and then step out of the way. Why should you have to travel across town and pay cash for the privilege of conferring with your guide when these visits are provided at home, free of charge, by the beneficent forces of the universe?

If you rely on a third party to mediate your psychic communication, you preclude the possibility of 3 A.M. encounters, sudden messages and warnings, and other information that might immediately prove helpful. The intermediary may overlook gestures and symbols which are significant to you and no one else. Furthermore, there's always the chance that she might be consulting not with *your* guides but with one of her own.

An intimate relationship—be it human/guide or human/human —is essentially self-sustaining. Once the two individuals have been introduced, outside intervention is seldom apropos and only rarely necessary (for the sake of support and clarification when the relationship gets bogged down). Psychic assistance has its place. But it's hard on a marriage when the house is full of "concerned" in-laws, even if they mean well.

How can you be absolutely sure whether or not an entity is a true guide? Couldn't a malevolent spirit strike a friendly pose?

A malevolent entity who poses as your guide will not communicate smoothly with you. It may be that he or she thrusts information upon you in an unpleasant fashion, or that the communication causes a pressure on your head, or that the energy field feels stressful, or that the contact leaves you exhausted and ill-at-ease. Somehow it's just not right. And the longer you carry on the relationship, the worse it gets.

Some spirits are tricksters. Others may wish to show you up for some reason. Still others may seek, through you, to rectify (or prolong) the negativity of a past-life antagonism. But as long as you approach the prospect of working with spirit guides in a positive fashion, the capricious or invidious entities will keep their distance. Fear is what opens you to negative interaction with a discarnate. Fortunately, to the degree that you're scared and self-protective, spirit contact is usually so scant that you're immune to input from any source.

In most cases, discarnate intruders try to approach you when you're going through some sort of dilemma. One time last winter I sank into a mire of worry, which I do now and then, and a household spirit began thumping around me. I told it to leave me alone, of course, and it did so temporarily. But as I went on worrying, it came back and thumped some more. Finally I started repeating a mantra designed to dispel anxiety. It also dispelled the spook. At this point I realized that the spirit's activity was just a means of mirroring my worry, getting me to see it for what it was: so much senseless thumping around in my head.

As a human being, you ultimately have to think and act for yourself, no matter how much communication you enjoy with the discarnate realm. It's you who has the opportunity—or obligation, depending on how you look at it—to decide which path to take, who to steer clear of, and who to get closer to, trusting in *how you feel* about each choice. You can't hand this responsibility over to your guides. You have to watch your own intuitive feelings and check them out thoroughly, then weigh them together with what you know about an entity's reputation.

I'm having trouble believing what my guide says. Much of the time I feel that her comments and observations are untrue.

Take note of the extent to which you trust human beings. Did you trust your mother and father? Do you trust the majority of people with whom you come in contact? Who do you trust more than anyone else in the world?

If you generally like people, you will like your guides. If you're filled with distrust, your guides will cause you no end of suspicion—partly in hope that you will overcome this.

Should you be ambiguous or overly suspicious about trusting others, try drinking herbal teas that are good for the lungs (mullein, sage, yerba santa). The lungs get affected by both sides of an exchange in untruth—when the lie is taken in as well as when it's spread forth. Yoga is also very helpful, especially since good books on yoga are readily available almost anywhere (e.g., *Integral Yoga Hatha*, by Yogiraj Sri Swami Satchidananda, or *A Child's Garden of Yoga*, by Baba Hari Dass). Kum Nye (a Tibetan system of health) and tai chi are equally effective if you can find a competent teacher.

Since distrust centers in the region of the heart chakra, don't limit your yoga to a pattern of exercises or a meditative ritual. Be sure to do the breath of fire and alternate nostril breathing. Experiment with any other breath techniques that your teacher (or book) might recommend.

All this attention to good breathing can't help but strengthen your lungs and chest.

When your system is in balance, you don't worry about whether or not you trust a guide. Either the trust is automatic and profound, or else it's not there at all. If trust is lacking, send the guide or guides away. Exclude them from your conscious sphere. In the meantime work on your self-trust—a second-chakra capacity—by doing the exercises outlined in Chapter 3. Once you learn to trust yourself, you'll find that trusting your spirit helpers will be easy.

Can I expect my guide always to look the same?

Asher, a guide who was a sage in his last life, works with hundreds of people. He appears in whatever accoutrements might be suggestive of wisdom. He has no need for the shepherd's crook that he usually carries, but many persons still respond to it as the emblem of a wise man. Once his contacts recognize the validity of his counsel, he drops the symbol.

Spirit companions do their best to figure out how you want them to look. If they initially arrive in a form that turns out to offend you, they'll endeavor to modify their appearance, usually without your having to ask. If they continue to change form while demonstrating consistency in other ways, they are no doubt trying to find a costume that you'll accept, cognitively and emotionally. One of my main guides, Johannah, used to come to me in middle-aged guise. Now she appears as an old woman. At the same time, in the course of recent work she's been doing with a friend of mine, she has manifested as a young adult.

One time a guide appeared and gave me an important message. She hasn't visited me since then, however. Can it be that this was not my guide?

Use your common sense. If the information she gave you has proved helpful or if life in general is changing for the better, she may be working in the background. Open up to her or call her by name. Ask whether she's still assisting you. If she fails to make her presence felt, you can rest assured that your original contact was transitory and that you're free to request another guide.

It's very rare for a life guide to disappear once contact has been established. In fact, during the initial period of getting to know you, they often cling to you. On the other hand, single-purpose guides almost always go their own way, though they might return at a later date if the two of you resume concurrent paths.

Every now and then I hear voices in my head—sometimes one, sometimes several—often rather loud and unpleasant. It seems to happen mainly when I go to the supermarket, when I'm sitting in a movie theater, or when I'm riding the bus. Are these the voices of my guides, trying to get in touch with me? Do I, for some reason, need the security of a public place in order for them to approach me?

The security of a crowd may appeal to you, but I strongly suspect that you're a psychic sensitive who is tuning in to the anxious mindchatter of others. It would probably be very good for you to practice the self-protective exercises that go with meditation (see Chapter 3). Re-invoke the protection throughout the day, especially just before you go into a public place. Do this for six months and see what happens. The voices will intrude upon you a lot less, and you can begin to send each anxious thought right back to its owner—with a bit of love and understanding, if possible.

What about cases of possession? It seems that we're always hearing about the spirits of the dead wanting to possess the living.

Possession is sought by beings who are on the outs with love. This is so whether the being is incarnate or in spirit. In fact, it's much more common to be possessed by some*body* than by a discarnate entity. Many a family (or business, or cult) is ruled by a parasitic personality who derives energy from manipulating and controlling the other members. It is revealing that some of the most manipulative people are the ones who make the loudest noise about the dangers of spirit possession.

Some spooks are earthbound, and simply desperate to talk to somebody. Others are confused, having died suddenly and/or violently. Do not fear these lost and wandering spirits. Ask your guide (or the universe) to arrange the proper help for them. Wish them well, but do not let them stay in your home or crowd you in any way.

Possession implies the inability to exercise one's free will. Your relationship with a guide includes the understanding that each final choice is always yours, even if the guide prefers otherwise and cautions you accordingly. Guides aren't permissive; they don't say, "Oh, do whatever you want, dear." Yet, except in certain life-and-death situations, they won't attempt to hinder you once you've decided for yourself. They won't demean your plans, nor will they sabotage your efforts.

A person who claims to be possessed is rejecting the capacity to choose and explore. Possession cannot occur unless people have already carved out empty spaces in their life and abandoned their own powers. The cure for possession is activity, creativity, a rich inner life, and renewed experience of God. A mantra can help begin to break down the negative pattern and restore self-esteem.

Guides belong to the orderly part of the universe. What gives shape and presence to demonic powers is the mind. Anything not from heaven is spun by the mind out of some form of fear. Dealing honestly and directly with one's fears is the way to guard against possession and obsession.

When I was about five I asked my mother if there was a devil, and she replied that her mother had always told her that there was a "trouble land," but no devil. To this day I believe that human beings fashioned the devil, and perpetuate its shadowy existence, in order to avoid taking responsibility for their own malicious attitudes and destructive behavior.

It's true that some guides would like very much to be in a body, just as some people would rather be free of one. Other guides have physical cravings that they hope to indulge vicariously: eating peanut butter, smoking cigarettes, being sexually inventive. Occasionally you'll get a guide who has past-life connections with somebody in your present life, connections that entail a certain amount of unfinished business that needs to be worked out. However, in the overall context of interacting with a guide, physical and emotional intrusions are usually minor wrinkles in the relationship, if they occur at all, and it's hardly ever a problem to define limits and set things straight.

How come my guide makes me uncomfortable, as if he's using me somehow or waiting to see whether I can squirm out of the situation he's maneuvered me into?

Your guide isn't supposed to make you feel uncomfortable on a regular basis. Some of your discomfort may stem from your own worry about what your guide might be thinking of you. The majority of our celestial friends have worked out their human negativity and have no plans to abuse us in any way.

Occasionally a guide may feel that you're not holding up your end of the bargain or involving yourself in too many unwholesome diversions: legal and/or illicit drugs, sex without love, gambling and gaming, workaholism, extreme socializing and excessive concentration on other people's affairs to the exclusion of what you need to do in life, or excessive reservation such that you fail to involve yourself in the outside world. The guide may stand there tapping a foot, putting out dirty looks and muttering words of reprimand in an effort to catch your attention. Or you might find the door to communication closed until you change your behavior.

On the other hand, a devout drunk told me that he could totally rely on someone else to drive his car home for him, no matter what condition he was in. His guide was willing to put up with his brazen demands for rescue. Although the man was in terror that he might someday lose the guide's cooperation, he refused to sober up and enter into the life tasks ahead of him. After several years he finally had a mental breakdown. At this point the guide acted very judgmental. There was much heated discussion as the man recuperated, and thereafter he learned to confine his drinking to wine at the dinner table. He and his guide now get along harmoniously.

If you honestly feel that a guide is judging you harshly and unfairly, ask him or her to leave. Every so often an entity will approach you in the guise of a guide, but will turn out to exhibit envy or anger. There's no need to feel that you have to help work out this kind of negativity, or be a receptacle for it, any more than you need feel duty-bound to perform a similar service for somebody on the earth plane.

Does the use of alcohol interfere with a person's relationship with a guide? How about other drugs?

All drugs that are processed or chemically derived—alcohol, cigarettes, cocaine, and so forth—interfere with the functioning of the sixth and seventh chakras. As a result, communication between spirit helpers and human beings is impeded. In addition, most people resort to alcohol and other processed drugs indiscriminately and excessively.

Natural substances in their unaltered state, when used occasionally and devotionally, may enhance our ability to interact with a spirit companion. Mindful of the importance of a sacramental purpose, Essie Parrish advised me to "smoke only when the spirits tell you to." She was referring to the use of a variety of angelica, which most California Indian tribes employ as a means for contacting their higher self. Other religious groups have, with positive effect, used peyote, cannabis sativa and indica, and certain varieties of mushroom as aids to discovering deep truth about—and in company with—their spirit allies.

I am pregnant. Could it be harmful to my baby if I contact my usual guide or meet a new guide?

Due to the interference generated by the fetal presence, pregnant women often have a lot of difficulty recalling past lives. At the same time, rest assured that an unborn child is not at all disturbed by mama's relationship with her spirit helper. Nor are little babies distressed when they go with their mothers to a spirit-guide workshop. On the contrary, newborns and infants who attend these workshops have bubbled and cooed with excitement upon the appearance of their mother's guide. The very young retain a direct connection with the other side of the gate, and they're delighted when their parent experiences the same sort of inner teaching to which they have regular access.

At the age of nineteen, pregnant with my first child, I made contact with our family guide and told her that I planned to name the child after her. (In those days I wasn't aware that our family guide already knew everything about us.) Right afterwards I went upstairs to lie down, and I felt the presence and movement of my baby for the first time. To my great joy, the baby went on moving and turning most of the night, as if to demonstrate her approval of the guided interchange.

I've heard that guides can manifest in physical form. Is this really possible?

Astrology is not only the life path but the livelihood of my friend Rio Olesky. Part of his earnings come to him by way of a class in astrology that he teaches each semester at Santa Rosa Junior College. The college is glad to have him as long as he draws a minimum of fifteen students.

At one point Rio ran into difficulty. His class was approaching its third session, and he had just fourteen signups. Since the college was adamant about the number of students, he was faced with the very real possibility that, for lack of a single signup, he'd be unable to continue the class in the future. His wife had volunteered to be number fifteen, and as he drove to class he considered taking up her offer, but it didn't seem right. "No, Rio," he told himself, "you're not going to stoop to that." Instead, he asked and prayed that all would turn out for the best.

As class began that evening, there were still only fourteen students present. Half an hour along, however, a woman suddenly entered the classroom. She was the epitome of a Madame Zenobia, dressed from head to foot in outlandish garb and carrying several large purses. She caused a great clatter as she made her way to the front of the room where Rio stood amazed.

"Can I give you the money now?" she asked, delving into one of her purses for the cash. Rio accepted graciously and showed the class a remarkable ornament on the side of the purse—an inlaid, mandala-like representation of an astrological chart, with all the major symbols. Then the woman sat down. But she didn't stay long, exiting noisily well before the session came to an end.

That was the last anybody saw of her. The woman failed to return for further classes. No one knew who she was. Nor had she been noticed anywhere around the county, though she would have stood out in a crowd of strange characters. Whoever she might be, she seemed to have come expressly to sustain Rio and reassure him in his work.

Aren't you being irresponsible to put out information like this? What if the wrong person got hold of it and misused it?

Unfortunately, there have been misusers of information since day one. Fortunately, the misuse of spirit-guide information generates terrible, terrifying karma—as numerous chronicles testify.

People prefer ignorance for two reasons: They're afraid of knowledge for themselves, or they're afraid to share knowledge with others, usually in order to maintain a position of power. In the long run, however, ignorance is always more dangerous than understanding.

According to the Old Testament, consulting with spooks or spirits of the dead is forbidden. I'm a Christian who believes in the Bible. How can I reconcile spirit-guide work with my religion?

This question needs to be answered on three levels. First, the Mosaic injunction against calling on spirits was made at a time when superstition was rife and spirit communication was dominated by corrupt necromancers. Numerous laws in Deuteronomy and Leviticus were designed to deal with the specific problems and health hazards of that long-ago period. Most of them have since been rephrased in the New Testament, or modified by Christian authorities and proponents of Reform Judaism, or abandoned entirely.

Second, if you feel that working with guides in any way erodes your faith or stature as a good Christian, then stay with prayer from the heart. It should be noted, however, that the Catholic Church has long held to the propriety of praying for help from discarnates who have been elevated to sainthood. Intercession may be requested for oneself or for somebody else. Catholics may also make offerings to saints, and some wear a medallion or other symbol representative of the canonized spirit.

Third and most important, as a practicing Quaker myself, I can report that my years of experience with spirit-guide work have only served to deepen and magnify my faith. Many saints and biblical figures have sought and received the advice of angels, who are master guides of a high order. The Holy Spirit disseminates a multitude of emissaries, myriad varieties and degrees of "angel." They all come from the same source and lead back to the same destination. Their ultimate purpose is to help you grow toward God. To this end, they may visit you only now and then. Or, if you wish, they have time and willingness to accompany you each step of the way.

To quote from one of the sermons of Phillips Brooks, nineteenth-century Episcopal bishop of Boston and a renowned preacher: "Certainly there is nothing clearer or more striking in the Bible than the calm, familiar way with which, from end to end, it assumes the present experience of the world of spiritual beings close to and acting upon this world of blood and flesh. . . . From creation to judgment the spiritual beings are forever present. They act as truly in the drama as the men and women who with their unmistakable humanity walk the sacred stage in the successive scenes."

9
HEALING WITH YOUR GUIDE

Self-Healing

In previous chapters we've alluded to guide-aided healing in connection with assuaging emotional anguish, but some guides can be particularly helpful when you have physical ailments as well. Emotional and physical conditions are interrelated. Colds, for example, can result from failure to express one's sadness. Since many of us have learned to repress feelings as a normal part of "adult" behavior, we're oftentimes unaware of the small grief that we're sick over. In this and similar cases, a guide can offer practical suggestions and perhaps point out the origin of the illness.

Let's suppose, on the other hand, that you have a chronic ailment, such as arthritis. Simply asking your guide to give you a healing may provide a measure of relief, but it's seldom enough to remove the condition more than partially, or momentarily. For a real cure to take place, the underlying cause needs to surface, and you need to take responsibility for it. Then you can begin again in a state of healthy balance.

This may not seem fair. In the misery of an attack you may turn inward to your guide and cry out, "Please, some help for these gnarled fingers and swollen joints—and for the anger and frustration that go with them."

At first the unfairness may seem compounded by your guide's unresponsiveness. But a few minutes later you're apt to find yourself crying; and when you finally dry your tears you suddenly realize that both the bodily pain and the frustrated rage have subsided quite a bit. This is frequently how a guide's healing works. Its purpose is not just to treat your symptoms but to open your awareness so that you can learn to heal yourself and/or maintain the degree of health that you now enjoy.

With improved awareness, you become more sensitive to other remedies—therapeutic apparel, certain raw foods, and a variety of exercises that can promote more lasting relief. Someone may tell you about a cousin who wears a copper bracelet. You might have a distinct urge to get into a warm bath (warm, but not hot) and to wrap the afflicted areas with wet washcloths. Or you may go shopping for groceries and find yourself drawn again and again to the apple juice shelf.

Confronting the same shelf for the third time, you might also confront your guide. "Did you bring me here so that I'd start drinking apple juice for my arthritis?" If the answer seems to be yes, ascertain how much you should drink and how often. Inquire if the juice-drinking is intended as part of a fast. Is it a temporary form of self-treatment or should it be incorporated into your regular diet?

A loving guide does not forget a heartfelt request. When you ask to be delivered from pain and frustration, you open a channel of communication, and over the next several months incidents long forgotten are likely to rise up for review by your conscious mind. As your guide knows, your conscious understanding of these significant events—and your capacity to make an emotional peace with them—are the means to permanent release.

By following your guide's advice, you may indeed free yourself from the bondage of a disease or an injury. And the cure may prove to be a lasting one. But overnight miracles are few and far between. In any event your guide can't heal you singlehanded—not on a permanent basis. As you go through life, you generate inner stress, stir up karma, and contribute to emotional crises involving others. Healing is therefore an ongoing process. A good guide tries to point you toward curative agents and procedures that will treat your present phase of difficulty.

Self-healing with your guide can involve major changes in the way you live. On the other hand, it may merely require a clarification of something you already know to be true for yourself. There doesn't have to be a physical or emotional crisis in order for you to be able to heal yourself or assist in the healing of others.

Lucien, a Hungarian refugee in his late fifties, was a farmer near a medium-sized town in Oregon. From his youth he had been well aware of his spirit guides.

He came to me complaining of leg cramps that woke him at night. I told him that his problem was not decalcification but dehydration, and that he should drink more water. In the small voice of a reprimanded child he said, "Is that why my guide always wants me to drink a second cup?"

Evan was in a marriage that appeared to be satisfactory and supportive. His wife arranged her own job so as to be home for him after work, and made everything as pleasant as possible. The two of them regularly went camping and skiing together. They discussed ideas and feelings at length and, in general, they seemed to take delight in each other's company.

Evan, however, was plagued with sore throats. Furthermore, on one occasion he badly injured his wrist while playing tennis, and the wrist didn't seem to mend properly. Although it was true that he and his wife got along very well on a superficial level, there was an underlying bone of contention between them, a deeper difficulty that had gone unresolved because they both persisted in avoiding it.

Evan came to see me about his continuing physical ailments. I realized that the problem was more profound than he was willing to admit, but I didn't quite know how to tell him this. Fortunately I remembered that, six or eight months previously, he had contacted a guide named Ching. And since Evan tended to gloss over personal unpleasantness in conversation with other human beings, I suggested that he turn to his guide for advice concerning his throat and his wrist. Evan had been working with Ching off and on, but it hadn't occurred to him that he could consult with a guide about something like this.

So Evan tuned in to Ching, and Ching reminded him that he was 34 years old and married for eight years, yet he kept on postponing the children that his wife was yearning to have. Ever since their marriage he had been placating her. "Wait until I get my degree." "Just wait till after I finish our house." He had even considered a vasectomy, but was afraid she might leave him if he went through with it. In any case, now was the time, said Ching. If there were to be any children at all, his wife needed to start having them soon.

Well, this information put Evan in a real quandary, and he got sicker than ever. But in the process, all sorts of hidden material began to surface for him to face up to and work out: his reluctance to be responsible to anyone, his inability to make deep commitments, his proclivity for hedging on a decision until the choice had already been dictated to him by circumstances. In the end he could see that if he wanted to be healthy, the solution was to interact with his wife in total honesty—to voice his fears, but also to heed her pressing desire for a child. Since middle age was around the corner for them both, he couldn't afford to sidestep the situation much longer.

Shortly thereafter, Evan's wife became pregnant "accidentally," and Evan spent the next six months sleeping in the spare bedroom, suffering from one contagious illness after another. Finally his poor health. began to affect his employment and his capacity for savoring life even to the moderate extent that he had before. Again he contacted Ching. Ching told him candidly that he was sick because he was still unclear about being a father, and that he was still unclear largely because once more an important decision had been made for him. However, Ching added, being sick was a useless form of avoidance. The child was bound to arrive.

"What can I do in the meantime?" Evan asked.

"Accept this aspect of your adult responsibility," Ching said. "Recognize your part in the parenting. With practice, you'll even learn to enjoy it."

This time Evan listened and made some effort to set things straight. He found that the more encouraging he was to his wife's maternal adventure and the more he gave of himself to preparing for a family of three, the better he *did* feel physically. But it was the birth of the baby that really began Evan's transformation. He found he could let the love of a new life touch the very core of his being.

Healing Others

In the middle of the night Sonia's little girl Abra got up screaming. Holding her, walking with her, rocking her, talking to soothe her —nothing helped. Baby aspirin was spit out immediately.

Sonia was just about to phone for assistance when she felt the presence of her life guide at her side. There came the message: "Put your hands over Abra's ears."

Sonia hung up the phone and did as suggested. Abra began to calm down. She stopped crying and leaned back against her mother. Following her instincts, Sonia carried the child into her bedroom, and the two of them lay down to sleep undisturbed for the rest of the night.

A guided healing of a friend or loved one is often as simple as the above. You act as a willing channel, and the other is a willing recipient. Sometimes, however, especially when working with people you don't know very well, you can encounter complications.

I used to be in an absent-healing group. We would meet once a week and tune in to sick or distressed people who had requested help. Whenever we felt over-burdened or under-energized, dissatisfied with our observational diagnosis or with the intuitive data we came up with independently, we would ask our personal guides or our master guide of healing to bring us a message. We would then pool our information, often discovering that we had received the same or similar material.

One of our clients was Anita Forbes, a teacher and practitioner of massage. Anita did very fine work, but her practice barely supported her because she charged too little. She weighed 275 pounds—much too overweight for her five feet, nine inches—yet she was a sensuous woman. She glowed with beauty despite the excess pounds. All was not well with her physically, however. She suffered from severe backaches and a persistent neck problem that could only be mildly relieved by acupuncture.

One member of our group knew Anita personally; the rest of us knew of her. Yet we were mystified by her ailments, sidetracked by her symptoms—her obesity and her spinal problems. None of us was able to see through to the underlying cause and provide Anita with information that would assist her to move ahead with her life. Having drawn a blank, we called upon our master guide Franco.

There was agreement in what we reported. Two members of the circle relayed the message that Anita's problems stemmed from her intense need to be in a loving relationship and to become pregnant once again; this tallied with what I received from Franco. In addition, my personal guide Johannah told me that, since Anita's two ex-husbands had custody of each of her children, she felt undeserving and undesirable, and this was why another chance at motherhood would be likely to restore her health. Meanwhile, the member who had introduced us to Anita's plight stated that she ought to leave her city environment and take up a more rural existence.

It was understood that whoever brought a case to the attention of our group would convey all the comments and suggestions to the person in question. Within a day or two, however, I stopped by at a friend's house, and there was Anita working at the typewriter. This was our first meeting.

"Well," said Anita, "what did your circle find out?"

"I'll let your contact person tell you the entirety of it," I said, "but these are my findings"—and I reiterated Johannah's message. Surprised by the reference to motherhood, Anita replied that her twelve-year-old daughter was coming from Nebraska for a long summer visit. The daughter had been living with her paternal grandparents, and Anita was feeling rather nervous that, having grown up in a small midwestern community, the girl might not care for an urban, West Coast lifestyle.

As it turned out, three months later Anita and her daughter moved back to Nebraska together. There, in her own home town, her massage business began to flourish almost overnight. The daughter was demonstrably glad to be living with her mother during her teen years. About the same time, the father of Anita's young son relinquished custody of the child for reasons of his own. So now she and both her children were under one roof. Over the past few years Anita has continued to be overweight, but she no longer has problems with her back or neck. She's full of energy and is a happy woman.

Our clouded perception of Anita was cleared up by requesting our guides to explain the origin of her difficulties. In much the same way, you can seek the aid of your personal ally when you're trying to find answers to your own riddles, or endeavoring to work things out with somebody to whom you're so closely attached that your perspective is bound up by your emotions. With spouse or parent, we're often so caught up by our emotional needs that we feel directly threatened by fluctuations in their mental and physical health. As a consequence it's hard for us (1) to see the contributing role we may have played up until now, (2) to discern the role that we should properly assume at the present time, and (3) to furnish data or clues that will really lead them to a clearer overview.

When your mate's physical condition or emotional climate is negatively affecting your own, sit quietly with your guide and talk the situation over. Usually the guide's response comes in words, though it's often given as a series of pictures. Not only will you receive information concerning the other person; you'll also get insight into how you can best put it across, so that your tone and the manner of your approach are in keeping with the effort to identify and treat the root of the discord.

When you are able to withdraw as one of the combatants in a family fracas and take counsel with your guide, you're more likely to re-enter the situation with an enhanced capacity for saying the right thing at the right time, and in such a way as to calm and nurture your loved ones. This recourse is of still greater importance when a family member contracts a life-threatening disease. Often we're so beset by fears of death that we effectively stand in the way of recovery. In cases like these, a guide can help us regain our perspective by pointing out the lessons that the afflicted individual (and possibly we ourselves) may derive from the experience.

Ramona, a 62-year-old woman who had recently retired from a

dynamic real-estate career in Albuquerque, New Mexico, suffered a near-fatal automobile accident. Her daughter Tessa, who had moved to the West Coast several years previously, came to me while Ramona was still in intensive care, hovering between life and death in a hospital over a thousand miles away.

Tessa was feeling guilty on two counts. First, she hadn't rushed back to Albuquerque as soon as she heard about the accident. Second and more profound, she felt that she ought to be living closer to her mother. Her ambivalence stemmed from the fact that she was an only child, reserved and self-contained by nature, and many times she'd thought she might be swallowed up by her mother's expansive personality. The only way for her to be a full-time artist, with the energy and confidence to support herself, was to keep a safe distance between them. Each time she had tried residing in the vicinity of Albuquerque, her mother would start urging her to join in some real-estate venture, or at least to take up something more solid than art.

I knew that Tessa had a guide, although she conferred with him only now and then. So after sitting and listening for a while, I said to her, "You've worked with guides before. I think you can handle this on your own." We reviewed the procedure for tuning in and making contact. Tessa grounded herself, and since we were sitting on the floor I had her put down an extra-large column from her first chakra. I also reminded her that when she did this at home she should burn candles and/or incense, to keep the room vibrationally clean and to prevent any unwanted energy-form from asserting itself.

Tessa then called her guide by name and he appeared. Since just the three of us were present, I suggested that she ask him out loud for a clarification of what she ought to do in regard to her mother. Naturally the guide already knew why he was being summoned, and with very little receptive difficulty on Tessa's part he explained that, essentially, Ramona was undergoing a life crisis. Her entire self-image had been bound up in her real-estate work, and she knew almost nothing of her spiritual potential. Fortunately, however, she had a devoted second husband. The auto accident (which she would survive) was appropriate because her husband's attentiveness as she went through the recovery process would activate a pattern of bonding that would improve their chances for a good marriage during their retirement years. As Ramona continued to recover, Tessa grew much less fearful of being parentally overwhelmed and was able to visit her mother in a more detached yet loving frame of mind.

A woman named Nancy, a nice, unpretentious person from a middle-class background, came to my office to begin a series of healings. Her symptoms were lower backaches that alternated on different days with deep, convulsive cramps in her upper back and shoulders. While menstruating, she suffered from excruciating pains, complicated by the fact that she was childless and had had her tubes tied. At other times she was unable to lift things because her shoulders were so tight and sore.

As she discussed her symptoms, I got an intense visual impression by way of my life guide. I pictured her ailment as a wave of sensation that surged periodically up and down the arc of her spine. The actual image that came to me was that of an ocean wave, first breaking on the beach, then pulling back. I could even smell and taste the sea.

A year prior to this, Nancy had embarked on a great change. Whereas her own family were all white-collar workers and intellectually inclined, she married a man who was a carpenter by trade and adventurous by nature, a man who was musical and imaginative and had tried out all sorts of new things. Four months after their marriage, the surging pains began. When Nancy ignored them and continued to work, their severity increased. At the point of her first visit to me (her husband was the one who sent her) she had finally quit working.

Nancy was a Capricorn. The rather conventional nature of Capricorns makes them reluctant to be innovators if this might cause them any social difficulty. Although Nancy had been reading numerous books on self-development and was willing to assert, for example, that one creates one's own reality, she still recoiled from other people's disagreement of disapproval. So she was in great conflict.

The first time Nancy came for a healing she appeared a bit frightened of the process, but the session proved fairly successful. Ten days later, however, she called me back and said that the pains were much worse; she needed urgently to see me again.

I expected to get adequate spiritual assistance for Nancy's second healing. But when I started to lay my hands on her in order to channel energy, I was told not to proceed. Instead, I sat down beside her on the bench and looked at her. There were beams of light radiating from the right side of her head and her right shoulder (right-sidedness denotes rationality). But on her left side everything seemed wrapped in cellophane, like meat in a supermarket just sitting there, inert. I began to talk to her about this in terms of her attempts to develop her psychic and intuitive capacities. She was quite open about her dread of the criticism that she felt would be forthcoming if she truly opened up in this regard. The only person with whom she had ever discussed such subjects was her grandmother, and that was infrequently.

I suggested to Nancy that, being a Capricorn, she approach psychic practice by way of methods that have already begun to be socially acceptable. As a means of explaining reality, she could familiarize herself with a centuries-old system such as astrology and consult with reputable astrologers rather than seeking straight psychic reportage. In an effort to improve her health, she could explore acupressure, acupuncture, and the principles of Chinese medicine.

Before marriage, Nancy had worked as an emergency-room nurse, and she agreed that certain alternative healing techniques had recently gained the tolerance of most M.D.s. She also admitted that she was drawn to astrology and numerology on account of their comforting exactitude, which made them seem valid disciplines for cultivating intuition. The color returned to her face and she began to breathe easily and rhythmically. As this went on, I was told to go ahead and heal her.

You have to be cautious about presuming to interfere in a process of disease or difficulty that someone else has set up for the sake of learning or to meet some other personal need. Even if somebody is bent on doing herself in, only a limited degree of interference is acceptable. As a consequence, in the role of healer, I often turn to the guides of my client or to my own guides for counsel as to just how far I may proceed.

A woman who had a large part in my training became quite ill with a tumor and seemed unwilling to go on living. Since she was past her three-score-and-ten, I didn't want to detain her if she felt that her work was done. At the same time, I was distressed at the possibility of her death and glad to learn that she had finally opted for surgery.

Tuning in to her and her guides, I found that she was chiefly in need of the close care that hospitalization would provide. She who had healed souls, ministered to the sick, and nursed the scarred beings that came her way now required an infusion of the same sort of energy, not only from the medical profession but also from the many visitors who would be sure to come see her.

Nevertheless, as I pictured her tumor, it appeared massive, unnecessarily large. Why not shrink it somewhat and simplify the operation? I couldn't take away what she had created for herself. But in the quiet of my mind I sent her love to do with what she wished, and the healing circle I worked with did the same. As it happened, the tumor diminished in size and she had an uneventful surgery. And as she desired, many friends came to visit and help her with her recovery.

When an ailment sets in as the result of a newly acquired habit or a temporarily upsetting situation, it's relatively accessible to treatment and removal. But when an ailment is karmic or inherited from a past life, it can be extremely resistant to healing. Although the sick person may be under the care of a competent physician, conventional or otherwise, although they may be benefiting from guided advice and assistance, although they may be faithfully practicing a diet, meditative regime, or exercise plan that seems to be succeeding, it's still very possible that after a while their negative condition will return, either as a life lesson or as a reminder each time they stray from their path.

10
BORROWING AND LENDING GUIDES

Borrowing Guides

In just about every personal relationship, the two people involved go through a blissful period and then reach an impasse, or else they adjust to a repetitive cycle of affection and animosity. Very few friendships, love pairings, and parent-child arrangements are continually joyful and supportive.

The same tendency holds true for relationships between human beings and spirit guides. Just because your guides are not on the earth plane, you can't expect them to be perpetual donors of unconditional love. It is true that, compared to a human friend, a guide usually continues to be much more respectful and loving when the two of you go through a phase of being out-of-sync with each other. My guides customarily indicate their disenchantment with me by falling silent. It's not an icy silence. They'll come and smile at me, but there's an ambience of reserve, of something held in abeyance.

A human/guide relationship is based on mutual benefit. Guides help you with your mission; you help them with theirs. Should you be unwilling to grow in a certain way or unable to carry out a particular service to humankind, it's understandable if they recede, or if they try to contact someone else to work with. On the other hand, when a guide fails to cooperate with you in a positive endeavor that you deem crucial to your life, it's perfectly all right for you to contact an additional guide temporarily or even to seek a replacement.

At the same time, one should keep in mind that a carpenter is not a plumber. Though well-versed in many respects, your guide is unlikely to possess universal knowledge and may know little or nothing concerning a phase of experience that you have questions about. As someone born and raised with an affinity for plants, you may have attracted a guide who was once a brilliant landscape gardener. He can steer you into the landscaping business and help you lay out the finest formal gardens in your county. But this doesn't mean that he knows anything about insurance or bookkeeping, or about the effect of mineral water on your kidneys.

Have patience. Make clear that you're open to further assistance. In some cases, your guide will confer with a co-being or a higher being and then deliver the desired information. In other cases, you'll be visited by a single-purpose guide, usually at the behest of your life guide. Meanwhile, the important thing to realize is that you can contact single-purpose guides on your own initiative. This often entails borrowing a guide who customarily works with someone else.

It might seem awkward to ask somebody else's guide for help, as if you were committing sinful trespass. But guide/human relationships are not exclusive dyads. If one of your friends has a guide whose talents are just what you need to solve a problem, you may approach the guide without an intermediary. You don't even need to obtain the permission of your friend. Guides are not indentured servants. They're free beings, able to ignore you, refuse you, or eagerly arrive to assist you.

A borrowed guide will help you determine how long the arrangement should go on. It might be a matter of minutes or months, depending partly on your need but primarily on the current requirements of the friend with whom the guide ordinarily cooperates. The duration of the arrangement will also depend on the guide's need to continue work left uncompleted from a previous lifetime or lifetimes.

Evelyn, a psychic colleague of mine, works with a guide named Hiroshin, who happens to have extensive knowledge in the field of healing. Evelyn and I used to participate regularly in a healing circle. As the group discussed someone's illness, she would often ask Hiroshin what he thought and defer to his advice—with good reason, since his diagnoses and prognoses proved to be not only correct but illuminating.

One day, after Evelyn had moved away to another area, I was presented with a client who suffered from a mysterious yet tenacious ailment. I decided to contact Hiroshin myself and ask him for the deeper truth. The client, a young man, had lost his mother at an early age and had recently been rejected by his longtime girlfriend. During a previous visit, I had seen liver damage that I felt was brought about by chronic fear. I sent him to a physician, in the slim hope that his ailment might be identified and treated medically. Such was not the case, however. His bodily troubles apparently stemmed from his negative emotional condition.

And so I requested Hiroshin's counsel. He didn't say anything, just sat there deliberating. But later that afternoon he brought me a solution. Wordlessly, he suggested a visualization exercise for my client, an exercise in imaginative concentration. I thanked him and he returned to his other activities.

At the outset of our next appointment, I passed on Hiroshin's suggestion. It worked. By mentally visualizing the clearing of his physical symptoms, the young man was able to begin moving them (both the symptomatic details and their overall pattern) out of his body and into his aura, his etheric level. From here, they could be much more ffectively disowned and easily dispelled. The visualization also enabled him to outgrow his emotional fix. Within a few weeks, his condition greatly improved. He found employment that gave him satisfaction and became involved in a mutually advantageous relationship with another young woman.

Some of you, even after having attempted the exercises in the preceding chapters, may still not feel that you have made clear contact with a guide of your own. When a participant in one of my workshops runs into this sort of difficulty, I give the person a guide to borrow for the duration of the session. The borrowed guide may be any of several beings, all of whom like to work with novices. Since I know them fairly well, I can usually select a guide who'll be compatible with the person I've asked them to join.

Assigning a borrowed guide may not always yield results, but it frequently succeeds where other approaches have failed. It's also a useful and pleasurable experience for class participants who have already gotten in touch with a guide by themselves. In addition, it gives me a chance to check on each student's facility for visualization and accuracy in receiving information and advice, based on the reports they make at the close of the exercise.

In one class, everybody took a borrowed guide and went outdoors to let their spirit friend direct them somehow. Anna, a gypsy being, was paired with a rather strong woman named Helen, who was scrupulously honest. Following Anna's lead, Helen took a walk through the neighborhood. She returned later than anyone else, giggling and disheveled, entering just as the last of the others was finishing up his report. Like a repentant child coming home to mama, she had a bouquet of flowers in one hand and a string of apologies to offer. She was late because she'd had to take back a ceramic frog that she'd removed from somebody's front lawn. Not only had Helen tuned into Anna's Romany clothes and looks, she'd also let herself be affected by Anna's attitude that one is free to help oneself to material objects. With a farewell to Anna, Helen put her back in the middle of the room, then sat there exclaiming, "I could never steal anything!"

Despite Anna's lightfingered ways, she will not help thieves; she'll only attempt to loosen up those who have a too-rigid attitude toward "mine" and "thine." Spirit guides may test your strength of character, but they are not allowed to mislead you contrary to your nature. In the meantime, the stronger and more firmly grounded you are, the less likely it is that a guide can even begin to turn you around. Just remember who *you* are; this is part of every successful friendship. Use your common sense and don't let yourself be indiscriminately swayed. Look to your conscience, your better judgment. You have to be able to say no.

As a borrowable guide, Anna's specialty is sudden weather changes. She'll cooperate, however, only for the sake of personal safety or the equivalent. She doesn't whip up storms to suit somebody's selfish or destructive whim. Don't call her unless you seriously need assistance in connection with the weather.

Basically, you borrow a guide for two reasons: (1) to have access to his or her field of knowledge; (2) to gain practice in guided work by interacting with a being who has a flair for communicating with people. Like Anna, the following "borrowables" are well-informed in one or more respects and are dedicated to helping you find and work with a guide of your own. You call them in the same way that you contact any other guide: by name and by intent.

Mort. A skier and runner. Able to assist with improving your agility and stamina. Also a psychologist who can help you to see beyond your mental smokescreens.

Ba. Appears as an Egyptian bird; has never incarnated. Brings messages relating to the development of one's mystical abilities.

Ambika. Little mother of the flowers. Willing to help troubled gardeners.

Joan. Tall, thin, and laughs easily. Died in a plane crash as a teenager. Wants to help younger people give shape to their potential and adjust to their adult dimensions.

Thomas Seton. A Quaker in Scotland in the mid-seventeenth century. He also appears as Lewis Sparling or Lewis Sterling, from a later lifetime. Will assist with prognosis and prediction in your personal life.

Munston. A master guide, glad to help anyone with cultivating non-attachment.

Wihambe. A South American Indian shaman. Will assist with astral travel provided that you have prepared correctly for the experience.

Blanche. Wants to work only with the elderly, the infirm, and those who suffer from isolation and loneliness.

Harry. A tax expert. Gives advice on financial aspects of business.

Esther. Coaches you in the contacting of a personal guide, and shows you how to be a guide's friend.

Mattuce. A travel guide, for astral excursions as well as conventional trips. Can provide assistance in connection with the mechanical problems of cars, trucks, and vehicles in general.

Steve. Can help you to see beyond the reasons for your behavior, so that you get a clearer and more precise view of yourself.

Kong. A teacher whose subject is the proper uses of power. Has a wonderful sense of humor.

Aarg. A potentate from an ancient culture. Can assist in solving sibling conflicts.

Blue Rose. An all-purpose guide who can help you to actualize ambitions and attract possessions if these skills are difficult for you.

Although the above guides have been of benefit to many people, you mustn't conclude that they're the answer to all your troubles. No guide can work even a small miracle in your life unless you're willing to put out your share of effort.

Borrowing a guide is an adventure in cooperation, trust and love. Remember as always that there's a delicate balance between stubbornness and surrender. Total surrender is salutary neither to you nor to the discarnate being.

It might seem impractical if not impossible for so few guides to fill dozens or even thousands of requests. Since they're not in physical form, however, they can be present in many places simultaneously, able not merely to converse coherently but to be fully aware of each person who has called on them. In fact, they may minister to several people on a regular basis.

In some cases, a discarnate being needs all its energy and is hard-pressed to multiply itself. Each individual is an energy pattern, and on the discarnate plane numerous friendly entities are permitted to imitate a specific energetic arrangement of knowledge, personality, and memory—thereby extending a guide's availability. As a result, what happears to be your guide may be a close associate filling in temporarily.

Almost anyone in the world of spirit can serve as a borrowed guide, even one whose co-being is presently incarnate. If your need is great and you wish to reach a particular person for assistance or counsel—whether it's your mother or Nikola Tesla or Eleanor Roosevelt—it's often possible to get in touch with them simply by tuning in to their vibration. A photograph or drawing of them may be an aid to tuning in, provided you realize that their own development has continued past the time of the picture.

Lending Guides

Love grows out of equal measures of rapport and trust. If you have a spirit companion with whom you feel confident and close, you can be sure that there's a great deal of love between you. And out of this love your guide will occasionally go watch over someone else when you request it, especially at a time when you consider the person's life to be in danger or their judgment to be impaired.

One word of caution. If possible, before you lend a spirit helper, have the borrower read Chapter 6, "Working with Your Guide." It's also advantageous if the borrower is able to ground and clear with meditation. A borrowed guide may be able to work with somebody who is confused and upset, but the hookup is much more likely to succeed when the person has made some attempt to calm down. People who are upset not only have difficulty listening and receiving, they also have a hard time revising their perceptions and behavior in the light of outside advice.

When you lend your guide to another, you don't necessarily deprive yourself. While on tour with someone else, your guide will return to your side at intervals, whether you broadcast a summons or not. In cases where they get profoundly involved and are unable to check on you personally, they'll send a proxy, a kindred being who can act as a substitute until they complete their assignment.

One of my best friends, Amy, was caught up in a custody battle over her daughter, a battle which she was losing. She was under such stress that she felt powerless to make realistic decisions about her life. Over a period of years, Amy had now and then observed the interaction that I carried on with Johannah, my main guide. Parenting had been one of the important activities Johannah helped me with. As a consequence, in the midst of her tribulation Amy asked me if she could have temporary access to Johannah's services. I told her I was willing, and that it was up to Johannah. That evening Johannah appeared to Amy in her most youthful form.

Amy's battle took all of Johannah's energy, and I missed her. I knew that other guides had the ability to act as her proxy, but I wanted only her. After a couple of months, however, having assisted Amy to secure joint custody of the little girl, Johannah returned of her own accord. There was no need for me to recall her because she never withdrew her primary allegiance. If you lend a guide, you can be sure that they'll come back to you, as long as your work and theirs continue to coincide.

Esther, described earlier in the chapter, is a guide of mine who likes to lend herself to people. One of these was Loretta, with whom she went home following a workshop. As Loretta told me later, she lost her temper at Esther for tagging after her. She even yelled and screamed, but Esther remained unruffled and simply went ahead with detailing to Loretta the various ways in which she could deepen herself and enrich her life. Upon recounting all of this to me, Loretta apologized for treating Esther so badly. "Apologize to Esther," I said. "I had nothing to do with the interchange."

Even in cases where you voluntarily lend or send your guide to help out another person, what goes on between that person and your guide is strictly their business—whether their communication be comfortable or difficult, extensive or insufficient. If your guide refuses to go off on loan, that's his or her prerogative. Equally, it's his or her right to leave you for a while and assist somebody else, whether you request this or not.

11
MASTER GUIDES

Master guides are spiritual beings who endeavor to implant seeds of higher knowledge on the earth plane, knowledge that is crucial for the given time and place. They interact with many people at once, helping to detoxify us of whatever poisonous notions of reality and truth we may have succumbed to. An infusion from a master guide may bring a fresh religious viewpoint into flower, as with the advent of the Society of Friends, who advocate pacifism and the love of a beneficent God—Christlike concepts which had become lost to many Christian denominations.

Master guides rarely channel for the sake of just one person. They stimulate individual creativity, but they focus on teaching those who will then go on to teach others. They also provide counsel and support for your regular spirit guides, to fortify their efforts in your behalf. Franco, a master guide who appears to me as a ball of blue light, comes to help in the healing of my clients. Once I asked him to do me a small favor apart from my healing work. He looked at me, laughed uproariously, and departed forthwith.

On occasion, however, a master guide will help out during the early childhood of somebody who would not survive otherwise, or someone who would grow up too damaged to complete the tasks that he or she has set up for this life span. An abused child usually turns out to be cruel himself. In nearly all cases, the capacity to transcend culturally learned patterns of destructive behavior is nurtured by exceptional guidance from spirit sources.

Susan was a self-effacing woman with a mousy, almost whiny, voice. During a healing session she told me that, when she was a girl, her father used to get drunk and turn into a verbal and physical tyrant at the dinner table, picking on each of the six kids one after the other for insignificant infractions. "Then," Susan went on, "one evening shortly before my tenth birthday, my father started in on his routine, and—I don't know where this came from, because I was a little scaredy cat who'd never done anything like it before. I stood up and said, in a loud, full voice, 'Well, I've had just about enough. That will do for one lifetime.' And I sat down again. My father was thunderstruck. He quit in the middle of his mudslinging and name-calling and, believe it or not, he never picked on any of us that way again."

Master guides give you aid and comfort if you're doing God's work on earth, living a life in which your best self harmonizes with the universal plan. Should you alter your purpose, however, and begin to misuse your power and talent, higher guides are apt to pull out in midstream and leave you flat—though if they especially care for you, they may instead pepper you with what we think of as "trouble" to help you see the light and mend your ways.

The technique for initiating contact with a master guide is the same as that for getting in touch with your regular spirit helpers. Ground and clear yourself as thoroughly as possible, then ask that the meeting take place.

Making the acquaintance of a master guide is not so simple, however. It's very unlikely, especially if you're new to spirit-guide work, that you'll encounter a master being merely by opening up once or twice—first, because the details of cooperation with a higher guide rely a great deal on the practice gained in working with regular guides; second, because it is the master guide who is generally in the position to seek you out, not the other way around. If you go chasing after a master guide, you're in for frustration.

A bright, overly ambitious woman who had studied briefly with me and others, began to teach her own psychic development courses. In one of her first classes, she decided to have her students experience their guides. She got them all into a fine meditative space, relaxed and open. Then, with the excess zeal of the apprentice, she directed them to seek the company, not of their everyday guides, but of the highest beings they could reach. To the woman's credit, the exercise elicited a response. Everyone in the class made some degree of contact and basked a while in the elevated energy. However, though instructed to do so, none of the students was able to repeat the contact during the week that followed. This wasn't at all surprising. Master guides arrive only on special and sacred occasions. Although the novice instructor didn't understand at the time, she was later informed by practiced teachers that her appeal to higher guides was inappropriate for a group of beginners.

By making full use of interaction with your regular spirit helpers, you raise your chances that sooner or later a master guide will choose to communicate with you. If the friendship of a higher guide is offered, accept with gratitude. The work you do in cooperation with master guides is filled with honor. In addition, a master guide will help you to figure out your true dharma, your own most righteous path through life, and will coach you to the point where love can flow through your heart. And when your heart is flowing with love, all other forms of personal fulfillment, including liberation from life's struggles, will also come your way.

In my own experience, meetings with master guides have been varied. Franco, the master guide who helps me with healing, came to me through my young friend Molly Klein, whom he was protecting. ZaHan, another master guide, hung around in silence, waiting for me to notice him; then he set upon me so heavily that our time together must remain on a back shelf until I convince him that being celibate is for discarnates, or until I'm old enough not to care. A conditional arrangement, even with a master guide, isn't always worth it when the promise of cooperation is offered in exchange for something you're not willing to give.

White Eagle, initially known to me as White Eagle Feather, is a famous master guide who assists thousands of people the world over. His name is symbolic, not personal. St. John the Divine was also known as White Eagle for his farsightedness and prophetic vision, and because he saw God's way so clearly.

I first perceived White Eagle in the flames of my fireplace as I talked to my Aunt Rose Spitzberg on the phone. During the previous week a spider bite had incapacitated my left leg from the knee down. The knee swelled with edema and red lines ran down my leg to the ankle: evidence of blood poisoning. Yet neither I nor the holistic physician whose office I shared could interpret all the symptoms, which changed from day to day. I was in frequent pain and exhausted by a schedule of nighttime teaching and daytime appointments. Several times over the course of the week the physician offered to take me to an orthopedic specialist, but I'm leery of doctors who restrict themselves to conventional medicine.

The day was approaching when I was slated to travel east to visit my family. Given the likelihood of making the trip on crutches, I called Aunt Rose. Although she was the best old-time healer I knew, I had hesitated to phone her because she was in her mid-seventies and in ill health herself. Aunt Rose suggested a few herbal remedies. These were remedies that she had taught me when I was a child, and I'd already tried them with little success. I was looking instead for the kind of intuitive diagnosis and healing advice that often came through her without effort.

As we went on conversing, I noticed a shape forming in the dancing flames of the fire—a figure *among* the flames but not *made* of the flames. It was an Indian man, straight and tall and proud, sitting on a horse. He radiated an aura of absolute self-command, as so many Indians did before their culture was destroyed. I realized that there was a connection between my Aunt Rose and this shamanic figure in the fire.

The next day I walked. I went bicycle-riding with my daughters and felt well enough to go for a stroll along the Russian River. My Eastern trip was pain-free and a pleasure.

White Eagle's interests center on bringing light to our planet. He does not act as a personal guide unless you are actively doing something in behalf of the light-bringing effort. Then he places himself completely at your disposal. He makes no demands upon you to alter your life habits; everything is on a voluntary basis and he's strictly non-judgmental. He's no fool, however. Either you carry on with your share of the work or he goes elsewhere. He may wake you at any hour of the night for a channeling—though if you insist on it, he'll also come regularly at an appointed time.

Franco, the other master guide with whom I've worked extensively, is much more in tune with personality changes and healing needs. As a result, he's apt to appear of his own accord when one of my clients has a problem he can address. He is very interested in the details of human lives and individual growth. And he's all goodness. If a malicious thought crosses your mind he'll chide you loud and long. His desire is that you stay in heart with everyone in your acquaintance, that you move on to higher and higher levels of compassion. However, he does not advocate the kind of selfless service that benefits others at your expense. On the contrary, he'll teach you a great deal about taking better care of yourself.

Once I asked Franco for a personal healing—the first time in five years that I'd done so. Within the day he let me see several times that I must remain true to my own values. Then he showed me seven things

I need to do to please myself. These are daily meditation and yoga postures, keeping a journal, writing about my work, gathering wild herbs, preserving food, and planting a garden. The last three are exercises in grounding. I have followed his advice as the seasons permit.

My experience is that master guides keep you company as long as the two of you are working toward a common end. Then they leave to find somebody else who will help them convert their particular quality and style of energy into an earthly reality.

Each master guide belongs to a tribal family,[1] related not genetically but spiritually. In analogous fashion, a master guide watches over a "tribe" of people related by the quality of their inner calling.[2] Sometimes a human tribe actually gathers in one geographical spot. In our culture, however, we're less inclined to band together. As a result a master guide may contact a scattering of individuals who begin to meet each other only as time goes on, recognizing belatedly that they have a common earthly purpose no matter how disparate their backgrounds and circumstances.

At all levels, spirit helpers have talents and interests that are the specialty of their tribal family: balance, courage, dependability, forgiveness, humor, kindness, dedication, sensitivity, strength. In dealing with human beings, master guides who share a specialty often partake of a single name. Each day hundreds of earthly requests go out to White Eagle, whose name has long been linked with psychic discovery. But the actual response comes from any of several score associates similarly competent to give advice on the matter at hand. The White Eagle clan is specifically devoted to encouraging visionary wisdom and to recharging spiritual belief systems. The focus of Franco's group is on healing and protection, and on the further goal of re-instituting love as the greatest healer and protector of all.

Right now there's a whole network of master guides putting their energy into raising and enlarging our knowledge of how the universe actually flows, and how love and freedom are intrinsic to this flow. It's for all of us to learn to use this knowledge so that the earth plane can evolve in its entirety.

Thus far in the twentieth century, master guides have been leading us in the direction of two major realizations. The first of these is that war is totally unnecessary and undesirable. Many people used to find war exciting and deeply meaningful, but it has become increasingly

---

[1]Master guides are also referred to as "ascended masters" and "elder brothers." An association of higher guides is sometimes called a "brotherhood" or a "lodge."

[2]Our vocational roles (pipefitter, writer, virtuous wife) are transitory; the calling of a master guide has permanence.

difficult for the governments of industrialized nations to convince their citizens to take part in armed combat. There's a rising global consciousness that human existence is a precarious boon that we all share, that the present world is in the midst of crucial change, and that any large-scale war at this time would be suicidal. We're beginning to understand that our real hopes, for survival and also for personal advantage, depend upon cooperation and mutual assistance.

The second major realization we're moving into is a fresh appreciation for the great importance of feelings and sexuality. Ever since the matriarchy fell several thousand years ago, people have concentrated chiefly on third-chakra work: power activities. These activities, and their external effects—including rational thought—have had a gradual culmination over the past few centuries. But in recent years the emphasis on power-moves and power-structures has begun to turn stale. We've begun to get involved with one another on a more advanced level: that of the fourth chakra, the heart chakra. We're discovering the value of letting out sadness rather than stirring it into anger (grief washes away anger psychically as well as physically). We're learning to express emotional joy, to exchange warm hugs with our children and friends, to recognize that feelings are vital, to know in our bones that life needn't be such a battleground. And we're finally starting to comprehend that sexuality is more than mere procreation or orgasm, that it can help us expand into the whole gamut of loving compassion, creative endeavor, and spiritual oneness with the universe.

The fourth chakra is the link between earthly humanity and cosmic humanity. Within us, the biggest and most difficult shift in quality of energy occurs between the third and fourth chakras. Once we're able to function fairly well as a "heart person" rather than a "power person," we move along much more readily to the development of full functioning in the centers that are still higher. Both individually and culturally, the energizing of the heart is pivotal. Love and compassion are indeed springboards to evolutionary ascent. In the meantime we continue to learn by way of first-, second-, and third-chakra experiences.

In general, our guides reflect not only our life calling but our level of being. Our level of being corresponds to the chakra(s) on which our life work is centered and also correlates with the aspect of self that we choose to emphasize. In addition to having chakras, we incorporate three essential aspects of self. The first is the basic self—our physical being, our raw emotions, our rational thinking, our belief systems and life roles. The second aspect, the middle self, is intuitional, creative and compassionate. The higher self is concerned with self-actualization, universal wisdom, oneness with all. These three aspects of the self constantly interact as a whole and with each other, regardless of the fact that, throughout our lifetime, we may concentrate on only one of them.

Although master guides pay emergency visits at moments of stress or peril, they're not likely to maintain close contact with you unless you're working at least on the level of the middle self. This takes quiet persistence, perceptive honesty, and a capacity to receive gratefully. There are creative geniuses—musicians, inventors, pictorial artists, and advanced psychics—who have master guides channeling through them regularly, because they've learned, each in his or her own way, how to work for the greater good of humankind.

Whatever your current level of being, a master guide who offers you friendship does so with the intent of bringing you to as much self-awareness as you can manage at the present juncture. Master guides also strengthen your creative courage. They cooperate with your particular talent and capability in an effort to trigger large-scale, long-anticipated changes on the earth plane, changes which fulfill their own aspirations for the planet.

The lessons of master guides are many, but their principal teachings revolve around love. Love is central; love is eternal; love is the most powerful of universal forces; love requires freedom to grow and thrive. It might not always seem that a master guide's influence relates to love. Invariably, however, people who link up with such wise old beings begin to appreciate themselves more profoundly and to demonstrate more kindness and scruple in their behavior toward others. A master guide is a loving gift, proof of the copious, everlasting care of divine consciousness. When a master guide taps you on the shoulder, trust that the the universe knows you're worthy, even if you yourself feel undeserving.

Archangels

The master spirits in touch with our realm are aided in turn by still more knowledgeable souls, all of them joined in a concerted effort to bring forth our noblest impulses. *Archangel* is the traditional term applied to these beings—beings of magnificent wisdom and enormous capacity to love—who oversee the workings of master guides.

Archangels are available to all of us, yet none of us can expect to summon them on demand. For the most part they visit and send messages only at times when their intervention is critical and providential. On rare occasion, however, they act as personal mentors to somebody who is having significant success in assisting others to advance humanly and spiritually—somebody who may or may not ostensibly be a spiritual leader or teacher. Those who attract a spirit guide of the archangelic order are notably discreet about their good fortune.

Sometimes archangels appear as illuminated visions. At other times they appear materially, in female or male form. Many gods and goddesses of antiquity were archangelic visitors. So were some of the most famous enlightened beings. Tales of gods and great beings are mega-concepts of the forces behind evolution, verbal attempts to codify the ways in which the universe works its power on earth.

The names of a few archangels are well-known because they have channeled information through persons who then became respected religious figures. Some archangels are also identified with a certain area of expertise, or with a certain form of governance—like Uriel, guardian of the akashic record, or Germain, "keeper of help" and guardian of the seventh ray, the direct line to the divine Source.

Though I've never had an archangel as a personal ally, one morning I was surprised to receive some input from one of their number. For years I'd been asking for information on how the higher levels of the spirit world relate to the earth world. The ensuing torrent of informational confetti, interspersed by my tentative questions, was the answer. I've tried to string it together in as linear a way as possible.

"We are the guide's guide, the Oversoul's resource person—although we can hardly be considered 'persons' as you know the term. Though similar to yourselves, we are of other orders as well as of the human order, and our numbers are infinite. We're not so confined as you are. We experience no separation between orders or dimensions of being as we do the work that is ours to do. Nor do we restrict the orientation of our energies to just one planet, just a single realm of existence.

"I have served and continue to serve in numerous capacities. Some of these are known to you and some are beyond your ken. I need no sleep and very little other renewal. I do take silent time for myself to rest and reflect, and every so often I seek some form of 're-creation.'"

Now and then a master guide assumes an incarnation, in spite of the freedom to refrain from doing so. I asked if, as I'd heard, archangels incarnate too.

"Only on particular occasions, and usually for a very brief period, not more than an hour or so at a time. We don't need to go through the process of being born to earthly parents; we simply appear as young adults or mature persons. We can also materialize clothing, a car, gasoline, and whatever else we might require. Temporary materialization isn't difficult for us, but it is exhausting.

"Most of our earthly manifestations are temporary. Once in a while, however, as one of several ways to reconstitute ourselves, we 'fall' to earth and become human in your sphere."

Why does a being like yourself—or any being—come to earth, I wondered. What's the *purpose* of living an earthly life?

"On earth everything about yourself can be inspected and interpreted in terms of duality: light and dark, old and new, good and evil. At the present time, dualities are the focus of teaching and learning on this planet. But the eventual purpose of immersion in a dualistic world is to show you that, in fact, dualities do not exist—that every so-called duality is actually a continuum, a unity. When dualities become gathered and absorbed into unities, the planet as a whole will advance to another level of consciousness; and there will be a change in planetary purpose, so that souls who have resolved the dilemma of duality can come back again for different kinds of learning.

"Your planet is a learning place, yes. Yet please don't get the idea that it's a penitentiary, or a 'reform school,' as one of your psychic researchers has termed it. It's far too pretty for that. I think of it as 'my beloved earth,' and all of us in my group cherish its endless variety of climate, topography and life forms."

I kept asking after the identity of my easy-to-read informant. There came this reply:

"You can call me 'the destroyer,' if you like—though the title refers to several associates whose goals are in accord. Our mission is to dismantle your outworn images and beliefs, so that you'll continue to open up your world's reality. To this end we sometimes use fire, which is dramatic as a psychic cleanser. In order to affect masses of people swiftly and tellingly we also use floods, earthquakes, freak storms, heat spells, drought, bumper crops, and come-from-behind victories by the underdog home team.

"It would be a mistake to emphasize the differences between your world and ours. There are many similarities, the social arrangement among them. On both sides of the veil you are part of a family, with ties of kinship. Furthermore you belong to a tribe-like group which specializes in a particular field of endeavor. Work projects in our world have effects and repercussions within yours, and vice versa.

"By telepathy the others in my group alert me to 'meetings.' We conduct our work in synchronicity, without the need to be actually gathered together. When I'm occupied, my associates try not to disturb me. Each of us has the benefit of a screening mechanism, and we hesitate to interrupt one another's privacy unless an emergency arises. In any case, even while resting, I'm able to stay attuned to all my involvements at once, sensing when my group is about to make contact with each other or with one of you. An earth body can manage only two or three things at once: carry on two conversations, for example, or chew gum, play the piano, and sing.

"Our work on earth is divinely directed and its performance gives us great pleasure, though by no means are all of us attached to the earth. There are other earth-like planets that we care for equivalently, planets with roughly the same vibration as yours. We accompany those with whom we share a specific part of our mission, on whichever planet they incarnate."

I asked how long this accompaniment lasts.

"For an instant, or for a lifetime. Anyhow, duration is relative. To be your lifelong companion takes only a fraction of our existence.

"When your work coordinates with ours, we do everything we can to help avert your troubles, even trouble that you arranged pre-natally or have due you karmically. As it is, much of your suffering is needless. There is a persistent and erroneous belief that any and all suffering is good for you. In fact, suffering does not always build character. Other aspects of experience are equally important if not considerably more so. Glorification of suffering is one of the outworn ideals that my group seeks to break up and eliminate.

"Another part of our task as undoers of old belief systems is to make sure that as many of you as possible have access to psychic tools and visionary experiences. We lend a great deal of support to those of you who are coordinating with us in this regard. Some of you made arrangements with us prior to birth; others have volunteered during the course of your present lives. A portion of you are members of human affinity-groups to which we've been assigned; the rest of you have chosen to develop talents and qualities of character in convenient agreement with our own.

"We'd like to assist you more often with choosing and deciding, but there's a fine line beyond which we may not interfere with your decisions. In addition, it's difficult for us to communicate with you directly when so many of you have been taught to be frightened of voices and visions, to treat us as if we were demons, and generally to prevent us from coming through. Perhaps we're more acceptable when we enter your dreams. Then, too, it's our preference to come to you when the din of the world is quieted by darkness, at midnight or in the still small hours before dawn."

I inquired: Are there any of you presently living among us in more than temporary fashion?

"Yes, a very few. But you wouldn't notice us unless we wanted to draw your attention. We're nothing like the fearful creatures from outer space that you used to be so fond of portraying in your movies. Our intentions preclude war and dominance. We do contribute extensively to your efforts at peacekeeping, however.

"We'd like to see less violence of all sorts. Earth has a couple of sister planets where most forms of intentional violence have ceased. There, in lieu of the excitement of power struggles, the population has worked on learning to levitate. Some of you would find this an appealing substitute for power games; others wouldn't. Accustomed as you are to the discordant intensities that you generate, you might not value a serene, secure atmosphere in which to cultivate further skills.

"Much of your violence is perpetuated by your system of giant nations—not a feature of our original design. It's true that we helped you to develop different languages, but we did so as a means of keeping you integrated within your own unit, your working affinity-group. These groups used to be familial, related by blood ties; the consequent cultures were tribal. Nowadays you tend to gather voluntarily, as friends, neighbors and scattered associates; the sub-cultures that result are more clearly based on affinity rather than on geographical birthplace."

I asked how a being gets off the wheel of birth and death.

"You quit working at it. Getting off the wheel is the by-product of a well-lived life. If it becomes a goal that you strive toward according to plans and methods devised by others, you won't attain it. Transcending the need to incarnate is an individualized phenomenon. It's not a skill that can be achieved by following a formula. So realize that gurus, sages, churches are only able to offer guidelines.

"Try also to understand that, before incarnating, you set yourself up for certain experiences so as to be able to grow in certain respects. In advance, you bargain like mad with your guides, your Source Self, and/or your Oversoul. Naturally you don't want the assignment to be too rough. Then, after you emerge in physical form, you do your best to open your mind and your heart, and to feel your way toward the broadest possible perspective. More often than not you do service to others and to yourself without even being aware of this.

"We intervene in your lives very little. But when we do, we create situations designed to nurture your highest mind. If you're poor we might make you rich, or we may provoke the opposite. Frequently you gain a valuable lesson as a result of accepting a condition and making the most of it, or as the result of laboring to reverse it. Although the lesson is sometimes lost in the process, our purpose is always that you reach out to realize the aims that you set for yourself prior to taking your present form.

"With our aid even a fool can become wise. As you know, occasionally the wise get lost and the low-minded acquire great intelligence. These are the kinds of developments that we foster in the attempt to stimulate you, shock you, encourage you further along your path.

"We enjoy being agents of evolution, helping to improve upon existing life forms. Earth is essentially a fine place to do this. Unfortunately your dominant culture has brought about the spread of techniques and habits which are ecologically unsound. We're currently influencing you to change in this regard—for example, to generate electricity by means of crystals rather than with fossil or nuclear fuels. I myself am particularly close to the fishes of the ocean and am filled with distress at how ruthlessly you've been depleting these creatures in recent years. For a while we reduced the spawning rates, to impress you with the effects of your short-term attitude, but indiscriminate and wasteful fishing practices continue. You also go on polluting the waters, as if this didn't matter.

"Your world is part of a greater and grander plan than many of you are willing to believe. We're at least as committed as you are to seeing it survive. The question is what form that survival will take. That will depend on the future you work out for yourselves and the efforts we make to advance all earthly creatures."

12
MESSAGES AND THEIR INTERPRETATION

For each of us the same words often have quite different meanings. When you ask for a message, your spirit helper may endow certain phrases and terms with singular connotations. Your companion also has to deal with *your* world view, which is idiosyncratic.

These difficulties are compounded by the fact that guides don't actually speak to you. Their seeming to do so is a function of your mind, which translates and extrapolates from the symbols that they send your way. All messages, whether auditory or visual or even tactile, are transmitted in symbolic form.

Why don't guides routinely step forward and communicate with full visual and auditory clarity? Once in a while it's because they wish to be cryptic, but mainly it's because the process of transmission between the spirit world and ours requires a personal wide-openness and a capacity for great effort, on their part as well as on your part. Both of you need to expand your perspective so that you see a more complete picture. Many guides are as hesitant as you are at the prospect of making conscious contact, and others lack skill in the procedure for sending symbols that translate into pictures and words you can readily understand. If you come away confused, go back and ask—as often as necessary.

Auditory Messages

In the spirit world, beings communicate directly, mind-to-mind. As you become able, even momentarily, to move beyond the customary human reliance on words and pictures, your guide can start to rapidly transmit thoughts in their entirety.

When you're just beginning work with a guide, however, you're likely to find that the easiest, most immediate way for you to receive messages is to hear a human voice. This voice may sound a lot like your own, and you may tell yourself that it's only the utterance of your thoughts. Then again it may have a distinctly different character —an accent, perhaps, or the tone of an older person, or the quality and pitch of someone of the opposite sex. Furthermore, as time goes on, the spoken advice may prove to be quite consistent.

If your fifth and sixth chakras are relatively clear and balanced, so that your auditory imagination is active and you're able to recall conversations and tonal qualities in detail, you are almost sure to hear messages with your inner ear.[1] When Evelyn, mentioned already in Chapter 10, was just beginning on her psychic path, she was out in her vegetable garden one evening transplanting some seedlings. She was feeling terribly agitated about a recent upheaval in her marriage, about the discomfort and uncertainty of her housing situation, about her unfortunate lack of capital, on and on. Working in the garden calmed her down somewhat. Suddenly, out of the blue, she heard an unfamiliar voice say, "Go to the Co-op" (one of a chain of supermarkets in the San Francisco Bay Area).

Evelyn had a tray of seedlings left to transplant, but since she was still feeling upset, she decided to go ahead and do as told. Dirty shirt, muddy hands and all, she jumped in her car and raced to the Co-op. Into the store she went, and over to the announcement board where a shaggy-haired man was just starting to tack up a rental notice for a two-bedroom apartment with a fireplace in the living room. Before the sign was on the board, Evelyn said, "I'll take it."

"But you haven't even seen it," said the man.

"Oh yes, I have," said Evelyn. "I used to be an Avon lady, and I know the address well." Later that same evening, she and her pleasantly surprised husband signed a lease agreement.

In many cases verbal messages are preceded or accompanied by a vague sense of music. On other occasions you'll hear a fragment of

---

[1]When people who have become physically deaf go into trance, they too are able to hear with the inner ear.

discernible song, perhaps with words to match the phrasing and rhythm of the notes. The combination of words and music doubles the auditory effect by appealing to both halves of the brain.

Now and then the music comes on *as* you're working with your guide, in the midst of a message. If so, this indicates that you are tuning in precisely and channeling correctly. It may also signal the further opening of one of your higher chakras (fifth, sixth or seventh). In any event, such music seems to herald an improvement in your ability to read clearly and to understand what you're receiving.

Roseanne, who was traveling out of state, agreed to look in on the relative of a roommate, somebody she'd never met. En route she kept hearing, by way of her inner ear, the words and melody of "All We Are Is Dust in the Wind." She assumed, quite correctly, that the person was dying. Another woman I know, an architect with psychic talent, routinely finds herself humming an invented phrase that helps her to solve some question she's mulling over.

At other times, the vehicle of communication turns out to be a line from a popular song that catches your attention as you listen to the radio or stereo. When you consider the words of the song as a whole, it may speak even more cogently to your present situation.

Back in 1967, my friend Natalie realized that she didn't want to stay in northern New Jersey, but she was uncertain what to do next. She was trying to decide whether she should go back to college in Boston or take a job that she'd been offered out in San Francisco. One day after work she started up her car, and since the radio had been left on, it began to play. The song went: "If you're going to San Francisco, be sure to wear a flower in your hair." There, she felt, was her answer. It proved to be a good one. Making the westward move and taking on the new responsibility opened up Natalie's life.

You may get messages by way of music without lyrics. A tune on a pipe or the wail of a harmonica can evoke the ambience of a significant life event that needs your reevaluation. A man named Paul used to hear the victory sequence from Sibelius' *Karelia Suite* whenever an adventure was about to befall him. Dvořák, Vaughn-Williams, and Mahler seem to have particular relevance for people going through an expansive phase in their lives.

Most of us tend to be more receptive to music than to any other communicative form—more receptive and less critical, less skeptical and doubtful. This is why instigating a song in your head and nudging you to turn on the radio at just the right time are two of a guide's favorite methods for tweaking your consciousness and bringing you to a moment of truth.

With musical messages there is also a tonal or qualitative factor. If you love chamber music and you get a message with a heavily syncopated upbeat, you're bound to have difficulty with it; messages need to be finely strung and gently rhythmic for you to pick them up accurately. Of course it's equally difficult for the jazz buff to receive a chamber-music message. The pace seems tedious, and he loses track of the sense and purpose.

As with verbal messages, your guide takes care to present you with qualities and styles of music to which you can react with pleasure and understanding. If New Wave rock disturbs you, your guide will avoid afflicting you with it (except, perhaps, to give you a jolt because you've ignored the mellifluous messages that she's been sending hitherto).

You may get tunes and lyrics that are completely new to you—possibly a repetitive chant or a refrain rather than a full-blown piece of music. These are your "medicine songs," for your personal use. Some are for healing. Some are for changing and growing. Some are just to make you feel at ease. And some are to tide you over during times of sorrow. These personal songs can originate in other ways, but spirit helpers are often the agents of delivery.

Your most important song is your life song. Each of us has a life song that is strictly personal and not to be sung in the presence of anybody else. Mine always precedes some sort of notable change in the matter or manner of my existence. Singing it, aloud or to myself, brings clarity, improves my endurance, and gives me new insights into my motives and needs.

If you don't know your life song, ask your guide for assistance. Get fully relaxed, ground yourself, and go inside to your place of inner quiet. Now make contact with your most trusted spirit helper and request to hear your song.

Let your song play you. Don't force it along. Stay open and receptive and allow it to flow through you at its own pace. As you listen carefully, the rhythm may alter. The tonal quality or even the tune may change. Continue to listen without straining. Concentrate on relaxing. Keep your breathing easy and regular.

Unless you have a good ear for music, you might not be able to vocalize your song until you've heard it quite a few times. Some life songs have words. The words may be in a language that you understand, either literally or sensually, or they may be enigmatic sounds. Other life songs are wordless. They come in like a symphonic motif, or a tune fragment, or even a nonmelodic line.

Visual Messages

Pictures

In answer to requests for messages, many people experience visual sensations—through the third or inner eye (the sixth chakra) as well as with the two physical eyes.

Try this as an exercise. Close your outer eyes and relax all the muscles of your face, especially around your forehead and jaw. The more you relax, the more your brain seems to become larger and larger, until it balloons against the confines of your skull. Now reach your perception into the corners of your mental expanse. Let your internal chatter fade and all other activity settle down; then see what emerges on your mindscreen.

You may be presented with a picture, or a sequence of images in storybook fashion,[2] or perhaps a moving picture. Accept what you're seeing; open yourself to the feel of its significance as well as the pictorial details. When a visual slips away, don't try to chase after it. Relax and breathe deeply so that you go further into trance. More visuals will arise of their own accord.

Sometimes the message conveyed by an image is obvious. Then again, a message may come to you only as the result of persistent deduction. It's also possible that there is no message, that the visual is simply for you to enjoy and let pass.

A meaningful visual has the same intense quality as a memorable dream. It could be the kind of dream in which you know exactly what's going on while observing the scene (and are even aware of pertinent data not revealed by the scene), or the kind of dream that shocks and mystifies you and from which you wake up all atremble and incandescent (the positive equivalent of a nightmare).

The dream analogy deserves particular emphasis since dreaming is another avenue of spirit communication. When guides can't get through to you any other way, they're likely to visit you while you're asleep, and you'll awaken with an image that ranges from scarce-remembered to crystal-clear. For the most part, such messages are sent three times, their delivery alternating between your dreaming state and waking state. It seems to take three repetitions for the tidings to clink-clink into one's cognitive awareness. As your receptivity develops, the repetitions become unnecessary.

---

[2]Although multiple images can be sequential, they can also be nonlinear, jumping from one fragment to another irrespective of time.

In all, there are four forms of intuitive envisioning. One is voluntary daydreaming: letting go and seeing with the inner eye, allowing a scene to be created before you.[3] The second is the nighttime dreaming with which we're most familiar. Then there's the flash vision that courses through your mind so swiftly that you stand there wondering what hit you. Finally there's the trance vision, which may be either a slight extension of your waking state or a deep inner journey that affects you profoundly.

Messages also come your way by means of objective visuals. You notice something, and for some reason it carries added meaning. You notice the bridge that crosses the river beside the town where you grew up, and you feel that you know very clearly where you're going in life. Up in Vermont on vacation, you're struck by a covered bridge that you've never seen before; you ask yourself, "What am I bridging at this point, and where does it lead?" At age twelve, thumbing through a women's magazine, I fell in love with the photograph of an eighteen-month-old girl with red hair and blue eyes. When I was a young mother, I looked at my own red-haired, blue-eyed child and suddenly realized the significance of the falling-in-love episode.

Browsing through a second-hand store, my friend Jack was drawn to a large print of a house on a hillside, with more hills beyond. The picture didn't appeal to him as a work of art, but after leaving the store he went back, made the purchase, and tacked up the print in his front hallway at home. A year and a half later he and his wife acquired an old farmhouse and a piece of country property which, though quite different from the scene in the picture, tallied with it in terms of topography and general ambience. He noticed the similarity upon unpacking the print at his new place. By now the picture had lost its meaning for him, and it went into a box of items destined for the flea market.

Although it's best to make the acquaintance of a spirit companion while in deep meditation, with your outer eyes closed, the relationship obviously becomes more practical as you learn to interact with your guide when your eyes are open. If you have to close your eyes in order to see or hear your guide, you make it hard for yourself to be presented with flashes, pictures, and movie segments under various other conditions well-suited to their reception: driving on the freeway, folding dry clothes in the laundromat, shaving at a mirror, weeding the garden, doing carpentry or yardwork, hiking in the woods, strolling up and down the beach, shopping in a large market, housecleaning,

---

[3]To send a message to someone else pictorially, consciously create the scene yourself. This is also a useful means for reprogramming your own reality.

cooking and canning. All of these open-eyed, routine activities tend to induce mild trance states in which you can reach your guide and your guide can reach you.

You might, for example, get a sudden recall of a once-familiar vista: a field stretching away from the back of the house. Or you might see a cluster of burning haystacks beside a lake, as if it were a movie clip. The picture may not have any obvious connection to your current thoughts, but something about it causes it to stick with you consciously. When this sort of thing happens, chances are that your guide is rescreening the scene so that you'll relate it somehow to a covert emotional problem or to an underlying question. Your guide may also slip you a scene from a past life, a panorama foreign to your present existence but that nonetheless elicits a great deal of feeling. Every so often your guide tries to alert you to a particular aspect of your total story, generally because it ties in with something you're living through now, perhaps for the third time, or the eighth.

Just because your guide's chosen medium of communication is visual, don't conclude that *you* are forbidden to speak. Feel free to make comments or ask questions as you see fit. Rarely will a guide resist this. Remember, at root they're not using pictures or words, but symbol patterns.

With a positive attitude you can gather strength from a visual no matter what happens. At best, you're the recipient of a message that's exhilarating and informative on several levels. And even when your first response is to feel shocked or perturbed, remember that you're in control, able to order the picture (and its sender) to leave the field of your senses.

Colors

Note the salient colors in the pictures that you see. If you receive a visual impression of your guide, pay heed to the color and style of the guide's clothing, hairdo, and so forth, especially if any of these features represents a departure from the norm. It's not significant that your leprechaun friend is dressed in a green outfit unless he ordinarily appears to you in brown.

A noteworthy blue suggests wisdom. Pink connotes love or affection and is often associated with information designed to open the heart chakra. Consult the color list back in Chapter 2. This will give you a key to interpreting the visionary colors that attract your attention. When a visionary color becomes luminescent, get ready for the vital and/or prophetic segment of the message. When the colors fail to impress you, they're just background phenomena.

Sometimes messages come through in a *field* of color. The whole scene is suffused in a certain hue. You see these fields of color with your inner eye, but now and then the impression is so intense that, even after you open your physical eyes, the color persists for several minutes before it gradually fades out.

Whenever you perceive a color field, take note of whether the color is one with which you resonate. Your basic color, more commonly called *essence color* or *soul color*, is the color of your being. It's not necessarily the same hue as that given off by your aura.[4] Your essence color represents the quality and tone of your inborn ability to observe and understand the universe—perhaps luminescent yellow-white, perhaps blue, perhaps red-violet. Usually, for the sake of good communication, you and your guide share the same essence color, or you have colors that are complementary. So if you're trying to contact your guide, look for an appropriate color to appear in your mind's eye along with any visual message that you're hoping to receive.

If the color field of a message is jarring to you (say, bright red, when your essence color is a soft blue) the transmitted picture will probably not come through very clearly. You may only get sketchy outlines. The entire scene may be obscured by the emphatic red tone, or the tone may seem so vivid that you end up merely reacting to it rather than attempting to absorb the message. Or else the images may change too rapidly or be too puzzling for your third eye to take them in.

---

[4]When you are most true to your Self, however, your essence color and the dominant color of your aura tend to be very close, if not identical.

There follows a chart of compatibilities and incompatibilities between essential colors and the color fields of messages.

Your essence color	Compatible color fields	Incompatible color fields	Remarks
white or crystal-white	all	none	Essential white and gold are neutral and can interpret well in any color field.
gold	all	none	
blue	green, purple, yellow-gold	red, darker oranges	Essential blue is comfortably centered but has difficulty with reds. Those with essential azure can actually feel pain until they adjust to a red vibration.
green	blue, purple, yellow-gold	red, all shades of red-orange	Essential green can be overwhelmed (browned out) by red or red-orange. Some greens also have trouble in the presence of light oranges.
yellow	blue, orange, red, green	purple	
lemon-lime	green, blue, yellow	purple, raspberry-red, lavender	Mentally well-organized. Becomes unbalanced in the presence of dark purple unless grounded and centered.
turquoise	blue, green, yellow	red-purple	
red-purple	red, darker blues	turquoise, azure	
pink, and other pale hues	cool, light colors	hot, heavy colors	Essential pink should take care to re-ground after reading through purples and reds.
brown, grey, or any tertiary shade			Essence color is being obscured somehow and is not coming through as it should.

Faces on the Wall

Every now and then the agent of a message is a face that suddenly appears as you gaze open-eyed at some sort of background. You may see it straight on or catch it out of the corner of your eye. Many people have reported the experience of encountering a face on the wall—a face suggested by the wallpaper or the knots in the wood or perhaps by nothing in particular. You'll also find faces in the leaves of a nearby tree, or in a section of broken-down fence, or in a cloud drifting overhead.

All of us, and especially children, enjoy discerning faces in a range of objects, from rock formations to piles of clothing to half-eaten ice cream cones. But noticing somthing that *resembles* a face is visual play. It's not quite the same as *seeing* a face, which carries with it the definite sensation of someone actually being there. A good test is to glance away and move around a bit, then look back. If the face reappears, it's very likely a form of salutation on the part of a guide who is keeping you company.

Some years ago a man named James came to me, disturbed about a series of monstrous faces he kept perceiving on the Japanese lampshade that covered the light bulb in his bedroom. The faces seemed to breathe menacingly at him. He'd see them before he turned out the light to go to sleep; and when he switched it on again in the morning, there they'd be. Then the faces began to follow him around. They would appear on the dashboard of his car and on the wall at work. He started to imagine that he was being pursued by demons.

Although James was in a desperate state when he told me what was happening to him, I didn't get the impression that the faces were hostile or demonic. As I said to James, it looked to me as if they were his personal monsters, guarding him from his own inner treasure. I felt that he had created them to keep himself from probing deeper into his life and finding his path.

James admitted that his current work dissatisfied him. He said that his family had always wanted him to be a professional man and that he himself found it unpleasant to act as a cog in the machinery of a large corporation. But he had no desire to be anything like a doctor or lawyer or teacher. His only real interest at the moment was sewing, in particular stitching exotic patches on pants and jackets, which he did occasionally.

I encouraged him to do more of this, and he agreed to try. Over the next few weeks he built himself an intricate cutting and sewing table, with a place for every scissor, spool, and implement of the trade. What he created was a marvel of cabinet work, innovative and one-of-a-kind. Other people saw it and exclaimed over it, and by the time I met with him again a couple of months later he was spilling over with enthusiasm for his newfound talent. He had even started to get requests to do remodeling.

I asked James about his monsters. He said that he was still seeing faces, but now they were generally of benign aspect. He'd noticed that if he was offered a remodeling job he ought to take, they appeared happy. If it was a job he should avoid, they would look cross or perturbed.

The repeated appearance of a face on the wall is often the beginning of a relationship with a guide whom you have not been able to contact in the usual ways. When a being has business with you—a desire to help you or redirect you or mirror you back to yourself so that you can make an advantageous change—the sudden appearance of a human face is an effective method for gaining and holding your attention.

Symbols

Visual symbols—geometric shapes, figures, and non-representational pictures—are important insofar as they mean something to *you*. If you receive an unintelligible symbol, simply take it in as best you can, without interrupting the flow of the experience. Then later on, when you have time for reflection, let your intuition help you to make sense of it. Or ask outright for clarification.

In our culture symbolic messages are necessarily individualized. Unlike so-called primitive peoples, we lack a consistent tribal symbology. Nonetheless, as our ancestors understood, the symbols that we envision are guide-directed or guide-amplified. Nothing in this highly intelligent universe happens without purpose. There are no accidents. As a consequence, if you don't catch a symbolic message the first time, your spirit helpers will try to slip it through by way of your dreams, or they'll arrange for you to meet somebody who puts the information into words that make you laugh and remember.

The symbols that you receive are often messages to grow with, coded knowledge for you to gradually unravel in the course of a lifetime. Some symbols are emblematic of the relationship that you have with your guide. You learn that whenever you see a bright triangular shape, the event has a particular meaning—just as when you hear a certain fragment of harpsichord music. Perhaps it's a portent of change, of a sharp turn in your path. Perhaps an achievement is imminent, such as the arrival of a new level of human understanding.

About the only symbol systems our society agrees on pertain to measurement and to everyday language. Yet there are a few symbols that seem to run through every culture on earth. Most of us, for example, accept that the sun symbolizes that which is male, assertive, and cognitive, while the moon represents that which is female, receptive, and subconsciously aware. As a result, when you're sick or distressed, your guide may present you with a moon symbol. The effectiveness of the symbol depends upon *you*, however. If a symbolic moon "hits the spot," the communication has been a good one. But if it seems inaccurate or fails to speak to you, feel free to question it or to request further clarification.

Numbers. We all have one or more lucky numbers, numbers to which we feel personally attracted and attuned. Numbers are therefore relevant to visual messages, both pictorial and symbolic. It may be that you see three rainbows at once or one rainbow three days in succession. In either case the number three might well prove meaningful to you.

Elinor was a young adult who, about ten years ago, was drawn to join a group of women doing guide-aided psychic work. On the evening of her initiation into the group, there were eight persons in attendance. In general an even number of participants weighs against the success of a ritual, but on this occasion a more important numerical configuration soon made itself manifest. When Elinor received her ceremonial gifts—a healing stone, a meditation pillow, and a handwritten book—seven stars appeared around her head, almost like a tiara. Everyone present perceived the same phenomenon. They took it to mean that Elinor would be an increasingly powerful teacher as she grew to full maturity.

The number seven is often thought of as fortunate. Actually it portends spiritual advancement. Ten years ago, Elinor was a vivacious girl in the thick of an active social life, and no one surmised that she would begin to seek long periods of time alone, away from all the delights of civilization. But this is precisely what took place. By now Elinor has indeed become a teacher in the discipline of her choice. She is capable, strikingly beautiful, and has great spiritual strength.

The following is a partial list of positive values and qualities traditionally attributed to certain numerical configurations and repetitions:[5]

1 Beginning; lone pioneering; individual will power

2 "Feminine" mentality (receptive intuition, ability to see two

---

[5]For further information on the symbolic values of numbers, see *Numerology and the Divine Triangle,* by Faith Javane and Dusty Bunker (Para Research, Rockport, Massachusetts, 1979).

2 "Feminine" mentality (receptive intuition, ability to see two or more sides of an issue); balanced, joyful constructiveness

3 Inspiration and truth; intellect; outspoken sociability; mothering and nurturing

4 Earthy security; worldly effort; capacity to organize and dominate; self-control

5 Learning and teaching; change and adventure; salesmanship; fearless ambition and aspiration

6 Love and generosity; domesticity; healing; social integration

7 Sensitivity to nature-wisdom and mystical wisdom; talent for artistic transmission of lofty ideas to the earth plane

8 Control of people and material goods; ability to communicate and to lead with understanding; capacity for using power wisely

9 Compassion and high ideals; service to all of humanity as a means toward one's own perfection

10 The number of God; the number of completion

11 Revolutionary thought; capacity for working with the building blocks of civilization and inspiring others to do the same

12 The number for an advanced state of mental organization, or for an advanced level of interpersonal organization (e.g., the Twelve Disciples)

13 A number of great power, within oneself or in a group; when thirteen sit in a circle for a specific objective, the power thus generated cannot be tampered with or shunted aside to the advantage of only one person (the Twelve Disciples plus Jesus)

18 Good luck and extra-long life (relevant to a situation, a project, or oneself)

22 Voluntary guru-ship: capacity for carrying out an extensive earthly mission, with harmony and balance as well as intensity of purpose

Creatures and Phenomena

People get messages in a great variety of forms. Some are surprising, if not extraordinary. Just as you're about to step into the street, you feel a tap on the shoulder; or you see a small rock fly off the sidewalk into the air in defiance of gravity. In either case you stop and turn around...and a truck runs a red light and whizzes past, missing you by inches.

Many of us find it difficult or threatening to deal with phenomena that are not of this world. As a consequence, guides often communicate by means of patterns and events that we encounter in ordinary fashion. You come home and absentmindedly switch on the TV, and the program tells you exactly what you need to know. While riding a bus, you read one of the advertisements above the windows, and it triggers your solution to some problem. You notice an odd shape in the clouds, and this reminds you of something important that you've neglected to do. You're walking along wondering whether or not to quit a safe but depressing job, and a whirlwind takes off your hat and tosses it up and away.

Animals and birds. It used to be, when everybody lived fairly close to nature, that wild animals and birds were frequent messengers. Nowadays, with urbanization widespread and much of the world domesticated, there is diminishing respect and affection for wild creatures, and much less opportunity to communicate with them and learn from them.

Since meeting up with animals and birds was once a common experience, pre-industrial cultures developed traditional codes for the interpretation of such encounters, assigning a consistent significance to the species of creature, the time of day, the day of the week, the location, and other factors. If you were walking through the forest on a Sunday morning and saw a stag before you on the path, this meant you were due for a marital or spiritual blessing. If a bird flew over your house from right to left, you and a friend would be parted; from left to right, you and the friend could expect to be reunited.

There were grains of truth in these explanatory systems, but the rigidity of the interpretations inevitably failed to keep up with the realities of a changing society, so they have fallen into disfavor and disuse, except among those who resist a modern education. Nonetheless, it's still possible to get an individual message from a free-ranging creature, even if you're a city-dweller and even if the creature is a pigeon or a stray dog. What matters is not that you see a particular animal or bird, or that it act in a particular way. The important thing is that you *notice* it, and you notice what it does. Creature and action impress themselves upon your consciousness. Most important of all, you connect the event to what you're already thinking about.

Let's say you're going through a period of arguing with your mate. On the morning of the third day you're sitting there in bed, and just as you're about to get up you hear a bluejay outside the bedroom window: "Yahh-yahh-yahhhh!" Then it strikes you that, on both of the past two mornings, there was a similarly noisy jay to razz you as you awakened. And this makes you stop and think, "Could it be some sort of announcement that I'm in for another day of squabbling?" Merely to think the thought is often enough to provoke a turnaround. You bid the jay begone and vow to conduct yourself with extreme discretion, if only to prove that you are master of your fate.

Derek was a young man who, though he loved the out-of-doors, found himself living and working in a suburban neighborhood of tract houses and shopping centers. One hot July he telephoned and asked if he could drive up to his friend Jack's twenty-acre farm and hang out for a while. Jack and his wife agreed. When he arrived he sat around for an hour or so, but before long he was on his way up the hill, gone exploring.

Derek didn't show up again until some time after dark. When he came in, he was both excited and bemused. Upon reaching the top of the hill, out of sight of human habitation, he had taken off his clothes and left them in the notch of an apple tree. Then he proceeded to investigate the open hilltop and the adjoining forest as if he were an animal, sometimes loping along upright, sometimes on all fours. Toward evening, at the edge of the forest, he caught something looking at him. He went closer and discovered a wildcat, with stumpy tail and tufted ears. To his surprise, Derek felt no fear. He squatted down and looked back at the big cat, and the cat continued to stare at him. It seemed to Derek that, in non-verbal fashion, the cat was trying to get across what the two of them shared. "At heart I'm part wildcat too," he explained, and went on to say that he realized he'd need to continue making a space in his life for this dimension of himself.

Insects. A bee can serve as a messenger, giving up its life to do so. Of course if you reach your hand into a patch of clover humming with workers, the message is obvious. But if you happen to get stung while inside a house at night, it might be a good idea to stop and take notice. The timing of the sting (in relation to events or to your thought process) and its bodily location are the chief clues to its significance.

Bees can alert you to danger, but they often bring good tidings, impressing you with the advent of something you desire. The swooping and buzzing of flies is less specific and less dramatic. Once in a great while a single fly will convey a message, but generally flies provide a background of sound, an approximation of the universal buzz of creative energy, and off this background you call up information that you're seeking. Crickets and other chirrupers make a very different kind of sound (in unison they produce a sleighbell effect, a jingling pulsation), but from this background some people are able to discern phrases in plain English: mainly advice and answers to questions. Though cricket messages may not bring inner peace, they tend to be prosperity-oriented.

Getting the Message

Even after a guide has arrived to heal you and deliver fresh hope for the future, you still need to feel deep down that you have the complete right to exist, and that you deserve all the assistance that spiritual and earthly beings can extend. Without this sense of self-worth, it's possible to take the most perfect gift from your life guide—or from one of the guides who helped ordain your birth, or even from a master guide—and neglect it or discard it, and resume your old habit of downgrading yourself. To a guide, this kind of circular, negative behavior is very discouraging.

Angus was a client of mine who had been in contact with a guide for quite a while. Sometimes during an office visit we would tune in on his guide together. One day the guide appeared looking as if he had been blinded. Neither of us understood that this was a message about Angus' own blindness. No matter what wonderful quality he was shown about himself, he went back to concentrating on his inadequacies, sexual and otherwise, plus his backlog of guilt and self-loathing.

For fifteen years the guide had watched Angus plod through life as if in a trance, numb to human relationships and mystified by them. The guide was even a witness when Angus got himself boxed into a corner and ended up having to kill a man in self-defense. Though the guide tried to forestall the terrible event, he couldn't. Angus had closed his inner ear. He just would *not* listen.

I soon learned that the guide was the principal force behind Angus' coming to see me. As a capable, responsible spirit helper, he hoped that I might be able to help trigger the insight that Angus resisted acquiring. He knew that Angus had to break with his past and start loving himself if he was to move ahead with his life's work. As things stood, Angus was on "hold." Although 52 years old, he was half that age emotionally, socially, and even intellectually. He still needed (and very much wanted) to find the right girl and get married and have children.

Yet Angus was also extremely stubborn. His desire to marry and settle down came second to his determination to stay stuck and confused. So when the guide again appeared to us without eye sockets, Angus once more refused to get the picture. As had happened before, the frustration was too much for Angus' companion to bear, and he withdrew.

A successful transmission requires cooperation. Guides do their best to put a message across, but you can't assume that their techniques of communication will be perfect. The efforts of Angus' guide, for example, were hampered not only by Angus' obstinacy but also by the guide's own long absence from a human point of view. He hadn't had a physical life in over 2500 years, and he couldn't really remember how to interact in depth with a flesh-and-blood person, especially somebody in a culture so far removed from the one which he last absorbed. His common bond with Angus was an enthusiasm for boat-building. Angus was a craftsman of small boats; the guide had been a master builder of Phoenician ships. They were able to share the tricks of their trade but not the secrets of day-to-day living. The Tibetans say that a being discarnate for seven hundred years no longer knows how to affect the earth. Seven hundred years has also been posited as the duration of a historical age, so the estimate may well be valid.

If you have a limited informational background, you may need to work harder to comprehend the messages that you get. Consider the following statement made by a guide: "To understand Jung, you have to look to your left." This message was received by a woman who had no knowledge of Jung or psychoanalytic thought. For her it was a mystery to be unveiled at a later date. Had she known something about Jung's work, it might have meant that at this point she ought to be using her intuition rather than her intellect.

An effort to rationalize a message from a guide often leads to obscuring it. Our rational powers constitute only about 10 percent of the mind's capacity. The less rational you are, according to conventional standards, the better you may be able to interpret a guide's communication. At the same time, if you give up your rationality, you won't receive as well or as much. To receive messages and to interpret them accurately, you need to be in a balanced mental state.

Extending the range of your knowledge and perceptual sensitivity can only help your understanding of the messages that come your way. Take advantage of guides in print—mythological stories, authentic fairy tales, Frazer's *Golden Bough*. And don't forget that trees, rocks, clouds, and the whole variety of creation exist in part as a metaphorical language to assist you with interpreting what your guides seek to tell you.[6]

---

[6]If you want to learn more about interpreting the significance of plants, a gooo reference to consult is *Magical Herbalism*, by Scott Cunningham (Llewellyn Publications, St. Paul, Minnesota, 1982).

13
DEPENDENCY AND OVER-DEPENDENCY

Guides are good and true companions, and it's easy to become over-dependent on them. This is so for two reasons in particular. First, continuing interaction with a guide can assuage loneliness in ways that human relationships rarely do. Second, your guides will play just about any role you ask of them. They're willing to stretch your success in almost any field of positive endeavor, whether you're seeking material wealth, fulfillment of desires, righteousness, liberation, or all four.

Most of us get hung up on the material plane, asking our guides to assist us with financial abundance, career advancement, and other wishes that can be met in the everyday world of objects. Our spirit helpers may implement this kind of request. However, since they themselves inhabit a world where thoughts create immediate action and reaction, they know that our ability to attract material treasures is largely limited by our fundamental thought-patterns, our concepts of what we deserve. Therefore they also attempt to provoke us and encourage us to move beyond our current material-plane illusions of limitation.

They might arrange an event that enables us to appreciate the moment for its own sake—for example, to enjoy the neighbors' swimming pool that we've been invited to visit for the afternoon, rather than to sit around feeling envious, coveting a pool of our own. In this way they expand our magnanimity, our human capacity, inspiring us to shed our pettiness and to cultivate greater tolerance and compassion for our fellow beings. And for ourselves as well. This is the kind of love that one develops on the path of *bhakti* yoga: the capacity to love ourselves and others without selfish motives, yet in such a way as to improve the quality of our lives. Bhakti-love is the matrix of most spirit-humn relationships.

Considering all that our guides are able to do for us, it can be a great temptation to allow them free rein and avoid making our own choices. But to follow such a course is always erroneous, sooner or later. If you're contemplating the purchase of a used car and your guide tells you it's the best deal in town, you should still take it to a mechanic. Acting independently is vital to your personal growth. By handing the whole decision-making process over to your guide, you neglect a large part of living your life. You have no center, no creative self. You're merely a puppet.

If you have a collection of antiques and your guide insists that you sell them, you have a right to know why. It may be that your attachment to them is preventing you from investing their value in something more stimulating to your existence, or that your fear of having them stolen has made you a stay-at-home unwilling to travel or even to attend local events. On the other hand, should your guide tell you to deal with your obsession by opening an antique shop, you might question whether you have the business skills to warrant such an experiment—even though it's very possible that you need to develop these skills, and to broaden your human understanding by interacting with customers.

Over-dependency is a danger to which most guides are sensitive. Seeing you show signs of weak initiative or indecisiveness, a guide of enlightened character will either inform you of this or withdraw for a period. Or both. Even your principal guide may close off from you for a while so that you'll start to exercise more self-reliance.

Respect your guide's intelligence about withdrawing. Conversely, make sure that your guide respects *your* desire to pull away for a while, if such is the case. In general, the only guides who might try to hang on to a person are those lacking a sense of their own developmental potential. Even with a guide of refinement and experience, however, you need to assert your independence now and then. A few months apart won't threaten a relationship meant to last a lifetime.

Sometimes, after long years of regular interaction, a guide will not only separate from you temporarily but also reserve the authority to re-establish contact. This standoffishness may seem arbitrary and unfair, but as a rule the guide has in mind your present shortcomings and the spiritual level toward which you're working. Your guides aren't likely to abandon you permanently, but they're quick to recognize the teaching value of more complete forms of solitude. True, there's a kind of solitude to be found in deep friendship with a spirit companion. But if you have a core difficulty to explore and work through—a personal pattern that acts as a drain, barrier, or stumbling block to your capacity for trust or power or self-respect—spirit counsel may be more of a hindrance than a help. Since your guides usually realize this, they're apt to fade into the background, restricting themselves to the role of careful observer until you generate the self-concentration to move through your difficulty and flow more easily and copiously with your own life.

Separation may also take place when a contact is meant to be of short duration. Guides often pick a person through whom they can channel a particular insight or piece of information. Because they do this is an egoless manner, the information comes out as the person's own. However, as soon as the result is made public, the guide will very likely bid you farewell—in part so that you will resume your work as an individual, rather than becoming enmeshed in spirit transmissions. You and the guide may be reluctant to part company, yet you can do so with joyful gratitude for the opportunity of having been there to serve each other.

No responsible guide will agree to change your destiny. Your karma is yours; it must be lived through. But *how* you go about this process emotionally and mentally has a great deal to do with its net impact on you, and here is where your guide can be of enormous help. In this and similar respects, successful cooperation between you and your guide is contingent upon each of you recognizing and understanding the limits of the relationship.

The impropriety of karmic interference works two ways. Discarnate beings have their own karma to live through, and for this purpose they have no more business relying on our powers than we do relying on theirs.

Keep in mind that, while guides have abilities we lack, the reverse is also true. We incarnate beings have powers that seem awesome and useful to them. Most notably, we have emotions—highly potent, bodily supported thought-forms that can crest into waves of sudden violence or dramatic demonstrations of love. The feelings we engender radiate energy into all the planes of our existence, and our emotional quality even bleeds through to the realm of spirit, giving impetus to our guides and other beings.

By contrast, the non-physical nature and the comparative sensory uninvolvement of spirit helpers make for emotions that are watered down, lacking in intensity and concentration, and therefore less effective as a motivating force. To compensate, guides have telepathic skills on the mental plane that far exceed ours. Here once again, we can focus on developing these skills for ourselves by means of observation and friendly emulation, rather than formalizing our dependence on the guide's telepathic superiority.

Your work with spirit companions gains in both expansiveness and practicality when you're able to retain a sense of overall balance, neither expecting too much of a guide's insight and wisdom nor allowing a guide to assume authority over your human potential. There are many styles of interaction that can leave each of you with the comfort of integrity and the power of choice.

Although mediums and psychics are commonly thought of as loners or even recluses, having contact with a guide need not keep you from broadening your social life or enjoying ordinary existence—as the rather extroverted authors of this book can attest. On the contrary, one of the chief benefits of negotiating a satisfactory arrangement with your guide is that you're able to apply what you've learned to all your human relationships, especially concerning matters such as who makes the decisions and who expects what of whom. Chances are that, with the people you have known for many years, you'll deepen your intimacy, your capacity for sharing. And any new friends that you attract are apt to meet you at least halfway in response to your current values, needs and desires.

14
COMPANIONS IN SPIRIT

*(A Transmission from Carole Judge
and Marie Le Casteau)*

A relationship between a guide and a human being is a two-way phenomenon. You may be attempting to contact us, but meanwhile we've been watching you for years and years, long before you were aware of our existence. Even prior to your birth we began checking out your life plans to see if you were the one we were looking for and if it was indeed our purpose to share in your development.

If you are a member of our tribal family and we made a commitment to act as your guardian angel during this life of yours, we'll always be within hailing distance. We may make contact only once in a while, but we do approach you periodically to see how you're doing. In the meantime, we try to arrange events that will help you to grow as a person, just as you yourself create events to stimulate your own growth.

Although we may not hover continually by your side, we are with you in your hours of deepest trouble, and we stay tuned to your life situation. You are never alone. Throughout your life you'll have company in everything of significance that you do. The universe may scatter its children far and wide, but it doesn't abandon them.

One of the main reasons you feel so alone in life is that you're too afraid or proud or uninformed to call out and ask for our assistance. We're always near enough to hear your request. If one of us cannot be of service at the moment, another will come instead. Solitary suffering is the result of insufficient faith. All you need do is ask for aid or advice, and one of our circle will be sent to shelter and comfort you.

By attending to your dreams, you'll pick up messages from yourself to yourself, and also from us. If you call one of us by name, we'll surely bring a ray of energy to help make things easier for you.

We can't always assist you as much as we'd like. There are those of you who have chosen rough assignments in this life. Some people seek to experience war, either to learn antipathy for bloodshed or to achieve the glory that they thought they missed in a previous struggle. A few may even elect to suffer a holocaust, as the Cambodians have recently done, to imprint forever on their souls the futility and stupidity that love's opposite produces.

As you advance your consciousness, many of you, in the United States and in other nations, are working toward peace. Keep in mind that peace is more than the mere absence of war. Peace has to do with respecting and loving everything alive, all of creation, and with respecting the many concepts of God that serve each of you in your own way.

Events are continually being created, by you and by us—to bring the Truth into focus for you, and also to bring you to focus upon the Truth. Your inner voice can steer you away from doing disastrous things to yourself and your fellow beings. The wisest part of you will be listening to this voice. When unsure, you can come to us for guidance or corroboration, and if your need is great enough, you may obtain help from an archangel or your Oversoul.

As regards events to come, most human beings are over-concerned with details of time and place. You tend to heed a forecast only if somebody says that it's due to happen on January 9 at 11 A.M. This is unfortunate. It is very hard for us to supply precise information about the future—first, because we know that such information contravenes your sense of free will, your power to shape your own life, and is therefore detrimental to your personal growth; second, because only those of us who have recently passed over are still attuned to your time schedule with any exactitude.

Dates and times are aspects of events that you do better to create on your own. When we say "now," we mean that the necessary conditions are currently set up for you to go ahead and be creative. When we say "today," we mean that, by giving your immediate attention to a possible event, you could make it an actuality before bedtime.

"Soon" is not a date; the event is suspended somewhere between the way you want it and the way we want it. "Later" is even less specific: it might never happen, or it could happen tomorrow morning, depending on whether or not you draw on the energy to enter into the event without ambivalence. In all cases having to do with the timing of an occurrence, it helps enormously if you can glimpse the hidden agenda of your life plan and if you can release whatever hold you might have on the status quo.

When companions in spirit furnish you with date and time, they're often being hopeful or even slightly manipulative; in other words, the actualization of the event is at least as important to them as it is to you. It's also possible that they're attempting to prove their credibility so that you'll trust them more profoundly. What we need from you is credibility. What you need from us is the assurance of faithfulness, of our continued good will and beneficent effect. What we need from each other is increased understanding and improved communication.

We can supply you with fresh energy and with ideas for renewing your life. We're always willing to help you develop contentment, faith, love, creativity, joyous self-expression and the flow of abundance. You in turn must be ready to permit these and all other positive qualities to manifest in yourself.

When you are on your proper path, doing the work that you must be doing, we give thanks, for your work and its success are also ours. Remember in kind to give thanks for the help that you receive. Like your earthly friends, all of us in spirit enjoy gestures of appreciation. Your thanks and praise come to us as affirmations that have much the same effect as the affirmations and visualizations you make in your own life. By appreciating us, you contribute to the fullness of our existence. Furthermore, you help us build the evolutionary mechanisms that allow reciprocal transformation to occur on both sides of the gate.

The "gate" is any access that serves to connect our domains. Each time you affirm and avow your beliefs in the reality of the spirit world, you open this gate a bit more, and your beliefs start to bloom into revelation and knowledge. Our discarnate home includes many planes of existence that not only complement but also vastly enrich existence in the physical realm.

There are four ingredients of transcendent living: prayer, meditation, love and forgiveness. Each of these works singly—and in combination, still more powerfully—to connect you to yourself, to other people, to the earthly world, and to universal consciousness whenever you feel abandoned and at odds. All four are routes to perceiving and appreciating the essential oneness of creation. The truth that rides above arrogance and guilt, blame and righteousness, is that we're all in this together.

To contact the author, write to:

Inward Journeys
P.O. Box 10204
Eugene, OR 97440

Tapes (45 minutes in length) of the meditation on pages 28-35 can be purchased for $12.95 (includes shipping and handling) from the same P.O. Box.

INDEX

Also by Laeh Maggie Garfield:

Sound Medicine
Music, single tones, singing, chanting, even silence—all of these can be focused and used for healing. This book explains the philosophies and metaphysics behind "sound medicine," then shows how it can be applied to everyday situations. *192 pages*

Available from your local bookstore or call (800) 841-BOOK for information on how to order directly from the publisher.

Celestial Arts
P.O. Box 7123
Berkeley, CA 94707